This Mighty Sum of Things

THOMAS J. ROUNTREE

# This Mighty Sum of Things

WORDSWORTH'S
THEME OF BENEVOLENT NECESSITY

UNIVERSITY OF ALABAMA PRESS
UNIVERSITY, ALABAMA

COPYRIGHT © 1965 BY
UNIVERSITY OF ALABAMA PRESS, UNIVERSITY, ALABAMA
Library of Congress Catalog Card Number 65–12244
Manufactured in the United States of America by
American-Book–Stratford Press, Inc., New York

"*The eye—it cannot choose but see;*
*We cannot bid the ear be still;*
*Our bodies feel, where'er they be,*
*Against or with our will.*

"*Nor less I deem that there are Powers*
*Which of themselves our minds impress;*
*That we can feed this mind of ours*
*In a wise passiveness.*

"*Think you, 'mid all this mighty sum*
*Of things for ever speaking,*
*That nothing of itself will come,*
*But we must still be seeking?*"

From "Expostulation and Reply"

# Contents

# Acknowledgments

As MY NOTES indicate, I am indebted to many scholars without whose earlier investigations this study of Wordsworth's belief in a cosmic benevolent necessity would have been a formidable and perhaps impossible task. To these scholars, including those with whom I sometimes disagree, I offer the genuine thanks that footnotes seldom allow—an appreciation for facts, ideas, shrewd conjectures, stimulation, and inspiration.

I am particularly grateful to the Trustees of Dove Cottage, Grasmere, England, and to their chairman, Professor Basil Willey of Cambridge University, for permission to publish Wordsworth's fragmentary essay in the appendix; and I am glad of a public opportunity to repeat my gratitude to the late Miss Helen Darbishire for giving me my first access to the essay. To Professor Lewis Patton and Duke University and to James Richard Scarlett, Lord Abinger, of Clees Hall, Bures, Suffolk, England, I am specially indebted for the use of Godwinian material from the Abinger Collection.

My primary thanks, however, go to Professor George W. Meyer of Tulane University, for it was he who first suggested to me the feasibility of this study and who directed my efforts at developing the material into a worthwhile dissertation. Because of the encouragement and "goadings on" with which he and Thérèse and Hudson Strode of Tuscaloosa, Alabama, favored me, I have had the enlightening good fortune to explore in detail one of the most fascinating Wordsworthian "elements of feeling and of thought."

THOMAS J. ROUNTREE

This Mighty Sum of Things

# ONE

# Introduction

In the so-called Great Decade (1797-1806) when William Wordsworth is conceded to have sustained his poetic creativity at its greatest intensity, much of his poetry states or implies a significant theme that has not yet received adequate investigation by Wordsworthian scholars. It is the theme of benevolent necessity, an optimistic concept of the world as directed inevitably toward perfectibility by a cosmic force that pays special attention to the educative effect of nature in the mental and moral progress of man.

Prior to 1797 Wordsworth was so well aware of the cruel and evil destructiveness of nature and human life that he had illustrated it vividly in his earliest poetry. In *An Evening Walk,* for instance, the wandering wretch of a mother, whose soldier husband has been killed at Bunker Hill, tries to shield her two small children against the cold and the rain, but the relentless elements not only kill the children but also flash lightning for her to see that they are dead against her bosom. *Descriptive Sketches* catalogues such evils as diseases, avalanches, wolves, storms, and deceptive mountain mists, which make prey of characters like the Grison gypsy woman and the Swiss chamois-chaser. "Guilt and Sorrow" points a blunt finger at war and forced enlistment which can leave a family destitute and in the aftermath reduce a good man to robbery and murder. And as if the outward forces of nature and society were not destructive enough in their direct way, they insinuate their deadly influence into man's mind as in Wordsworth's lines entitled "Incipient Madness" and "Argument for Suicide."

In spite of the seriousness and prominence of these subjects among his early preoccupations, however, in 1797 Wordsworth began following "principles of selection and emphasis" which enabled him to celebrate "only those aspects of nature and humanity most likely to encourage the development of the benevolent or social affections, and to accelerate the decay of the malevolent, anti-social passions." [1] Corresponding with this new selective method was Wordsworth's belief in a benevolent necessity, which did not become prominent in his poetry until the same year of 1797. Quite probably it was this belief that called forth the new principles. The belief would have been the initial thematic basis and the new principles the permanent method in Wordsworth's new-found purpose of justifying, like Milton, "the ways of God to men." The present study plans to examine this thematic basis in Wordsworth's poetry of the Great Decade (1) by presenting evidence that, in addition to his personal experience, Wordsworth found intellectual support for his belief primarily in the writing of William Godwin and of David Hartley and (2) by comparing his treatment of the theme with their treatments.

In summary outline Wordsworth's theme is relatively simple. A concise and limited definition would make a distinction between benevolent necessity and determinism *per se:* whereas determinism means that any development has to be what it is, either good or bad, benevolent necessity means that all development is toward good. If a man's past and present influences have inevitable results that tend toward moral and social betterment, that man is directed by benevolent necessity. What appears to be a development of evil consequence is really only one stage in a movement toward a greater good. In its simplest definition, then, Wordsworth's theme is that of deterministic meliorative influence; but the details are quite complex. A review of the scholarship that has touched upon the theme indicates that almost no one has gone beyond a statement of the simple outline.

Among Wordsworth's contemporaries, Coleridge and Hazlitt were well aware that Wordsworth's thought had its necessitarian phase. Coleridge himself had early advocated and then denounced the doctrine of necessity.[2] In a letter of 1804 he wrote that he had convinced Wordsworth, who "was even to Extravagance a Necessitarian," that it was a "pernicious Doctrine." [3] The letter does not say when Wordsworth held his extravagant belief or when Coleridge dissuaded him from it, but

Coleridge's use of the present perfect tense and his ambiguous explanation of the "sophistry" of necessitarian arguments suggest that his refutation had been recent and that he still felt a need to clarify his position. In reality, Wordsworth was not as fully persuaded as Coleridge thought in 1804; however, the point here is that Coleridge simply states, rather than investigates, Wordsworth's belief.

The same is true with Hazlitt. As a headpiece to the 1814 essay "On the Doctrine of Philosophical Necessity," Hazlitt misquoted from "Tintern Abbey" (lines 92-102) and paid the following compliment to Wordsworth: "Perhaps, the doctrine of what has been called philosophical necessity was never more finely expressed than in these lines." [4] In *The Spirit of the Age* of 1825, writing an essay entitled "William Godwin," Hazlitt thus illustrated the general enthusiasm for Godwin's *Enquiry Concerning Political Justice* during the mid-1790's: "Truth, moral truth, it was supposed, had here taken up its abode; and these were the oracles of thought. 'Throw aside your books of chemistry,' said Wordsworth to a young man, a student in the Temple, 'and read Godwin on Necessity.' " [5] In the essay "Mr. Malthus," Hazlitt, again identifying Wordsworth's belief in necessity with Godwin's philosophy, said this of the latter: "The hopes and the imaginations of speculative men could not but rush forward into this ideal world as into a *vacuum* of good; and from 'the mighty stream of tendency' (as Mr. Wordsworth in the cant of the day calls it,) there was danger that the proud monuments of

time-hallowed institutions . . . might be overthrown." [6]
Hazlitt's remarks are significant in directing our attention to Godwin as an influence on Wordsworth's belief
in necessity, but they give no indication of the content
or complexity of Wordsworth's thought about the subject.

Another contemporary, De Quincey, seems to have
noted only the "inevitable prosperity" in Wordsworth's
life: the legacy of Raisley Calvert, the final payment of
Lord Lonsdale's debt, the bit of "fortune" that accompanied Sarah Hutchinson when she became Mrs. Wordsworth, the legacy at the death of her uncle, the stamp-
distributorship of Westmoreland, and the later addition
of part of Cumberland County to the Westmoreland
district.[7] Like Hazlitt, De Quincey is useful in pointing
to the importance of events in Wordsworth's life that
shaped the poet's thought and feeling; but only the first
event mentioned by De Quincey came early enough, in
1795, to help crystallize Wordsworth's creative impulse
into poetry about benevolent necessity. This event combined with other early occurrences to direct Wordsworth toward his new-found theme of 1797. However,
since De Quincey's discussion of inevitability did not
press beyond Wordsworth's life into his poetry, De
Quincey is less helpful than Coleridge and Hazlitt in an
exploration of Wordsworth's belief in necessity.

In 1879 Matthew Arnold said of Wordsworth, "His
poetry is the reality, his philosophy . . . is the illusion." [8]
Yet in spite of Arnold's dictum, critics and biographers
have continued to value that philosophy. While empha-

sizing particular philosophic aspects, most of them have
rested content with relatively little detailed discussion
of the doctrine of necessity. They have, I believe, relied
too heavily on Coleridge's early letters—particularly the
one of 1804—and have decided that, since Coleridge began voicing a distaste for necessitarianism as early as
June 1796,[9] Wordsworth slavishly followed and soon re-
canted. These critics have generally failed to note that in
his *Table Talk* of 31 July 1832 Coleridge revealed the
original design of Wordsworth's *Recluse* (with which
*The Prelude* and *The Excursion,* both composed later
than 1796, were integral) as one of Christianized necessity. Wordsworth was to treat of man and nature, of
pastoral and city life, and of

> the present state of degeneracy and vice; thence he was to
> infer and reveal the proof of, and *necessity for,* the whole
> state of man and society being subject to, and illustrative
> of, *a redemptive process* in operation, showing how this
> idea *reconciled all the anomalies, and promised future
> glory and restoration* [italics added].[10]

Since Coleridge felt that this was in substance what he
had been trying to do all his life in his system of philosophy, it would appear that he had never gotten rid of
necessitarian elements in his own thought. If he is right
in crediting this design to Wordsworth, then the greatest
bulk of Wordsworth's poetry was motivated by necessity, either philosophic or Christian. His early form was
primarily philosophical necessity with Christian coloring, and it permeated more of his poetry of the Great

Decade than modern critics have hitherto acknowledged or demonstrated.

It is only fair, however, to note that critics writing after Arnold have mentioned Coleridge's and Hazlitt's references to Wordsworthian necessity, and some have detected isolated instances of it in the poetry. In 1897 Emile Legouis made passing reference to it without pursuing the subject among the poems.[11] Arthur Beatty, who in 1922 demonstrated beyond doubt the influence of David Hartley on Wordsworth, stated briefly that the belief in necessity is found in *The Borderers,* "Guilt and Sorrow," "Tintern Abbey," and a few early-written lines of *The Excursion.*[12] Beatty is certainly correct in noting some form of determinism as a theme in these works, but he makes an apparently contradictory observation about *The Borderers:* while deeming the villain Oswald the protagonist of the play, he says that Oswald is a kind of Iago to whom "every fresh step in criminal conduct appears a justification of the one that preceded it, seeming to bring again the moment of liberty and choice." [13] Determinism and choice, however, are inimically antithetic. In ascribing the theme of necessity to *The Borderers,* Professor Beatty may have been thinking of Oswald's statement in Act III (lines 1560-1567) that the faintest breath can move a world or that the sneezing of a cat or falling of a leaf might prevent a thing from happening. All this, though, is purposeless determinism used in a sophistical argument to turn the hero Marmaduke from the idea of remorse. The passage certainly indicates Wordsworth's interest in necessity, but what

Oswald expresses is not the teleology of a *benevolent* necessity.

Similarly, "Guilt and Sorrow" may be read as an instance of negative social determinism that brings unwarranted misery to the sailor, the female vagrant, and others, but this determinism is not set within a greater framework of philosophic necessity. Whatever may have been the intended effect upon the reader, within the poem itself I find no suggestion that human misery is suffered for an ultimately good purpose. Consequently, though a kind of necessity is at work in the poem, it is not a benevolent kind. The adjective in the term *benevolent necessity* sets a thematic limit that excludes both *The Borderers* and "Guilt and Sorrow."

When Beatty brought out a second edition of his book in 1927, Melvin M. Rader almost immediately pointed out that there were limitations to the Hartleian influence on Wordsworth, including "Hartley's doctrine of optimistic necessitarianism." [14] In 1931 Rader discussed the subject of Wordsworthian necessity again, citing Coleridge's letters and the lines Hazlitt had misquoted from "Tintern Abbey"; but after suggesting a parallel with Spinoza's determinism, he remarked: "We may surely say that the general tenor of Wordsworth's thought is quite opposed to necessitarianism." [15] As an example he cited "Peter Bell," quoting the lines about nature's inability to touch Peter's heart with "lovely forms." This, of course, is not the whole story of Peter Bell. The outcome of the poem does lie within the realm of benevolent necessity (see chapter five).

Perhaps the most interesting criticism of Wordsworth's belief in necessity is that of Hoxie Neale Fairchild. In 1931, with important qualifications but
without textual investigation, he made sweeping statements about the omnipresence of the theme in Wordsworth's poetry:

> In fact it is possible to say that at every stage of his de-
> velopment Wordsworth was chiefly dominated by neces-
> sity in various guises. From 1793 to 1796, it is necessity
> in a more or less purely Godwinian form. From 1797 to
> about 1805, it is necessity in the guise of nature, suffi-
> ciently tinged with transcendentalism to surmount the
> logical difficulties of his nature worship and to raise it
> above its foundations in eighteenth century science.
> After about 1805, his sensuous descendentalism begins
> to fade and his conservatism begins to grow. Necessity is
> now Duty, "stern daughter of the voice of God," the
> "new control" mentioned in *Peele Castle,* but really the
> old control in a new form.[16]

In reference to benevolent necessity I question Professor Fairchild's first two sentences because Wordsworth's early work like "Guilt and Sorrow" shows only
negative social determinism and because Godwin's philosophical necessity from the first edition of 1793 is posi-
tively optimistic. Otherwise the critic's observations
strike me as sound. However, by 1949 Fairchild apparently reversed his stand, for he wrote flatly that
"Wordsworth had not been 'even to extravagance a necessitarian' since 1796 at the latest." [17]
Miss Helen Darbishire has devoted the most specific

study to Wordsworth's belief in necessity. In 1948 she gave a concise examination of eleven poetic passages (composed mostly in 1798) and one prose paragraph (of 1810) and concluded that Wordsworth's idea "involves the paradox that to live according to the order of Nature is to be free." [18] Her investigation implied that Wordsworth's belief was limited to the time when he was meditating the philosophical poem to be called *The Recluse*—that is, primarily during the year 1798. Within two years after her 1948 essay, however, Miss Darbishire seemed to have extended her evaluation. Although she presented no new evidence, she cited Wordsworth's "adherence to the doctrine of necessity" as one of the three most important and basic ideas in Wordsworth's thought:

> These three strands in his thought seem to be, of many strands, the most important, and they are naturally interwoven in the form as well as the content of his greatest poetry: the vital significance of sense-experience, the assurance of the mind's intuition of the infinite, and a conviction of the inevitable, resistless movement in nature and man towards some unseen spiritual goal.[19]

Despite this assertion, Miss Darbishire added no further proof or illustration of Wordsworthian necessity. In fact, in 1952 when she published her second edition of *Poems in Two Volumes, 1807,* she made no reference to necessity in her discussion of *Lyrical Ballads* and the poems of 1807.[20] Apparently she either assumed it was not germane to the short poems or did not then consider it important enough to add to her original introduction of

1914. Miss Darbishire, like Fairchild, had stated the importance of Wordsworth's doctrine of necessity, but like him she seemed to have lost or minimized her convictions about it.

The fact remains that, while numerous scholars have referred to it,[21] Wordsworth's theme of benevolent necessity has not received adequate investigation. It is difficult to explain this comparative neglect unless it be that, because of the repeated assertions of belief in some form of benevolent necessity by post-medieval scientists, philosophers, and poets, the general source and content of Wordsworth's theme have appeared too obvious to merit extended, analytical study. If such is the case, however, it represents false reasoning. Wordsworth's conviction about benevolent necessity is too important as a major frame of reference underpinning many of his greatest poems for it to be taken too easily for granted. Likewise, the primary influences that led to that conviction are too specific to remain unexplored now that enough evidence seems to be at hand. It is in the sense of meeting a need, then, that the following pages attempt to localize these influences and to delineate the poet's thematic conviction. Such an attempt should strengthen an appreciation for the complex synthesis of Wordsworth's poems of the Great Decade.

# TWO

# The Preparatory Milieu

JUST AS WORDSWORTH himself realized and stated in Book II of *The Prelude* (1850 version), it is a hard task to analyze a mind, even one's own. The difficulty is that the mind, insofar as man's methodology permits him to examine it, is at any present moment the result of an incremental past which with obstinate reluctance only now and then reveals to the analyst its more significant accretions. Hence it is that, in sifting the known facts for the developmental pattern of Wordsworth's belief in a benevolent necessity, one seeks and finds pertinent influences that suggest the fullness of his mental growth and final conviction on the subject of necessity. His personal experience and the influence of Hartley and Godwin are the most specific and immediate determinants and therefore the most significant. Nonetheless, the belief in necessity after the sixteenth century is important as part of what Joseph Glanvill would have called the "climates of opinion" in Wordsworth's day, and it is appropriate to look briefly at this background, but primarily to illuminate the fact that for twenty-seven years of his life that background alone was not enough to stimulate him to the point of writing poetry about benevolent necessity.

### SCIENTIFIC, PHILOSOPHIC, AND POETIC BACKGROUND

Since the new science of the Renaissance threatened to relieve the universe of its God unless the new laws of nature could be shown to derive from God, many defenders of Newtonian science turned the discoveries of Kepler, Galileo, Newton, and others into cosmic exempla of God's benevolent forethought.[1] But science nonetheless took its toll of religion. With God conceived by some as a kind of grand mechanic who had set the world in motion and subsequently left it alone to follow its mechanical laws, man took three attitudes that were direct attempts to meet the new science and its implications, either to combat the science or to absorb it. Basic to each attitude was the concept of an *anima mundi,* an idea that behind nature lies "something far more deeply interfused."[2]

One attitude of man enabled him to accept the incontrovertible evidence of science and at the same time keep God functioning within His created world; this compromise led to deism, which in turn often approximated pantheism. In spite of its gigantic success in making the universe scientifically understandable, geometric mathematics shook the foundations of man's metaphysics and religion. For example, Descartes, though he gave ontological proof of God, lessened man's status in the new cosmology when he separated mind and matter as disparates; and Hobbes was able to resynthesize all things only by declaring that all was basically material, even images of the mind and ideas. Newton's scientific demonstrations of gravity, mass, and motion, and Locke's emphasis on experimental knowledge strengthened the growing materialism of mathematical science. Nonetheless, many of these thinkers, feeling the need to adjust science to religion or philosophy, postulated a supreme being that was a great mechanic who either had set things in eternal mechanical motion and then relaxed merely to watch or had started the interrelated worldly mechanisms and remained among them to insure their working according to the mechanistic plan. In either case, the world followed a mechanistic plan of necessity, and the providence of the great mechanic was generally considered to be benevolent.[3]

Another of man's reactions to science was a strengthened religious fideism. The abstract quality of mathematics and the "naïve faith" in the possibility of science left room for faith in a necessary order of things.[4] But probably more important was the reaction of men like the Cambridge Platonists against the extreme materialism of Hobbes. While arguing for the supremacy of spirit over matter and for the identification of God with the extension of infinite space, Henry More assumed the beneficence of his extended God. John Smith based his rational faith on mystical experience as a means to divine knowledge, and Ralph Cudworth conceived God as Mind that was senior to the world and "the cause of all other things." [5] Underlying these attempts to justify religious faith against materialism was a sense of the overall purpose of God. Rational ways of understanding and explaining God were possible because God had ordained them in His creation of the world and thinking man.

Man's third attitude was a fideistic tack that reached toward a Shaftesburyian concept of the goodness of man. Before Shaftesbury there was the Protestant emphasis on the authority of the Scriptures and on the individual's right to interpret them; the growing mystical impulse of Protestantism inculcated faith in the Inner Light and in individual human goodness. [6] By making a synthesis of the universe known to science and the beautiful forms found in the external world, Shaftesbury combined the secular and religious in his concept of the goodness of man. While insisting on the unity of all objects in "a system of all things, and a Universal Nature," the animating principle of which is the deity, Shaftesbury was persuaded that "the order of the world is good and guarantees the goodness of every individual life if taken in its connection with the whole." [7] *The Moralists* addresses a panentheistic "Author and Subject of these Thoughts" that moves "all Things" with "an irresistible unweary'd Force, by sacred and inviolable Laws" framed for the good of the individual and the perfection of the whole; the "vital Principle" is everywhere and is shared by all. [8] The tenor of Shaftesbury's diction and the capi-

talization of certain words indicate an uneasy fusion of
Newtonian science with the religious Godhead, but they
also indicate recourse to a benevolent necessity as an explanation for the world. The goodness (God or vital
Principle) in man both derives from this necessity and
enables man to comprehend it. And others did comprehend it, for on through the eighteenth century Shaftesbury's moral-sense theory and benevolence influenced
moralists such as Francis Hutcheson and Adam Smith to
view the world as animated in all its details by a benevolent necessity.[9]

These three post-medieval attitudes toward a world
newly shaken by the discoveries of mathematical science
overlap, but more importantly they agree on at least one
significant point: a religious or quasi-religious *anima
mundi* operating in terms of benevolent necessity. In all
three points of view the world-activating principle—the
Great Mechanic, God, or God as goodness in man—is
seen as benevolent and in some degree purposive.

Such prevalent ideas might well have reached Wordsworth either before or during his days at Cambridge
(1787-1791). For instance, John Jebb and other Cambridge lecturers emphasized God's benevolence in estab-
lishing necessary laws for all heavenly bodies and for
nature in general.[10] However, since at college Wordsworth
was only a desultory student and since scholarship has in-
dicated that we cannot be as certain about his early non-
poetical readings [11] as we can be about the poetry that his
poems echo from the very beginning, it seems worth-

while to note that some of this poetry contained these attitudes toward benevolent necessity.

The references for "universal benevolence" in the first two volumes of Fairchild's *Religious Trends in English Poetry* will impress a reader with the prevalence of the theme in eighteenth-century poetry. Both volumes indicate that benevolence was expressed poetically from a number of points of view—fideistic, deistic, philosophical, metaphysical, political, and social—and often enough as a combination of these views. Stemming from Shaftesburyian philosophy and usually voiced in deistic terms,[12] the idea of universal benevolence assumed a tenor of providential necessity in the poetry of men like Sir Richard Blackmore,[13] William Falconer,[14] James Grainger,[15] and Robert Nugent.[16]

Among the poets whom Wordsworth read in his youth, Alexander Pope believed in "the great and fundamental principle of this law, universal benevolence," [17] and James Thomson relied heavily on "the doctrine of cosmic benevolism" in *The Seasons*.[18] In "Spring" (lines 849-866) Thomson says that God, "this mighty breath" that instructs the fowls of heaven, with boundless spirit and unremitting energy "pervades / Adjusts, sustains, and agitates the whole," the "stupendous scheme of things." [19] As Wordsworth was to do three quarters of a century later, Thomson sometimes juxtaposed to his fideistic attitude a belief in the melioration of the human mind ("Summer," lines 1800-1805, and "Winter," lines 605-608) and a sense of mystical joy in contemplating the goodness and contentment of "Creative Bounty"

("Spring," lines 867-903), a joy very much like the later one which Wordsworth often voices in *The Prelude* and the loss of which Coleridge laments in "Dejection, an Ode." Thomson's general emphasis, however, is on the teleology and the final cause of the created universe, for behind all nature, good and wise, sustaining and animating the harmonious whole, is God. Wordsworth was to delve more deeply into the efficient cause, the empirical proof of the *modus operandi* of benevolent necessity.

Subsequent eighteenth-century poems that Wordsworth read in his youth stressed a benevolent necessity: Edward Young's *The Complaint; or, Night Thoughts* (1742-1745), Mark Akenside's *The Pleasures of Imagination* (1744), and James Beattie's *The Minstrel* (1771-1774). With strong overtones of Newtonian science, Young's belief was that, since heaven transmutes evils into "moral goods" ("Night IX," lines 377-392), all nature is involved in benevolent and necessary interrelationships ("Night IX," lines 696-707) that lead to inevitable progress: "From purer manners, to sublimer faith, / Is nature's unavoidable ascent" ("Night VII," lines 1347-1348); "Nature delights in progress; in advance / From worse to better" ("Night IX," lines 1958-1959).[20] Part of this progress depends on man's mental ability to "half create" what he sees in nature ("Night VI," lines 415-441); but man's creative mental power, coming from heaven "of strict necessity, not choice" ("Night VII," line 1293), derives its immediate stimulation and strength from the Creator's great natural objects ("Night IX," lines 1059-1064). Hence, it is man's "sov'reign duty" to half create the nature that he finds, thus reciprocating and aiding all things—including himself—in the general progress toward a "millennial love."

In "The Design" of *The Pleasures of Imagination* [21] Akenside carefully points out "the benevolent intention of the Author of nature in every principle of the human constitution." Book I of the poem itself says that God's providence made man's soul capable of enlarging its view of the immense chain of being "Till every bound at length should disappear, / And infinite perfection close the scene," a conclusion stemming from "the eternal growth / Of Nature to perfection half divine." Book II expresses benevolence in terms of God's precise, scientific plan of nature, while Book III states the providential correspondence between nature and the mind of man. The incomplete Book IV illustrates that in the "dawn / Of life" nature "fix'd the colour of my mind / For every future year." Throughout the poem, as he writes of nature, mind, imagination, and passions, Akenside reverts to the overriding theme of Godly benevolence and the perfectibilitarianism of the divine design.

Beattie's *The Minstrel* [22] describes benevolent necessity in quasi-religious terms of science and deism. Refractory man is cautioned not to rebel against a necessity that glances at Newtonian science: "shall frail man heaven's dread decree gainsay, / Which bade the series of events extend / Wide through unnumber'd worlds, and ages without end?" The reason for caution is that, of "the whole stupendous plan," man dimly scans "one little part." Nonetheless, kind nature, liberal but not lavish, works toward the "soul's eternal health" because "all her schemes with nicest art are plann'd, / Good counteracting ill, and gladness woe."

Since universal benevolence was an accepted belief in the eighteenth century,[23] and since necessity was concomitant with benevolence in the poems of writers known by Wordsworth in his youth, one might expect him at least to refer to the concept of benevolent necessity in his works that precede the possible influence of Godwin and Hartley. But not until 1797 [24] does he both state the concept and develop it as a major theme in his poetry. However, before the evidence for Godwinian and Hartleian influence on Wordsworth's theme is examined, it is important to note attitudes and concepts in Wordsworth's early life and poetry that preclude any inconsistency in his development of this theme in 1797. This background can be readily condensed into a consideration of Wordsworth's general optimism, his personal experience with benevolence, and his empirical naturalism.

WORDSWORTH'S CONCEPTS AND ATTITUDES UP TO 1797

Wordsworth's optimism began when his idyllic early life and education in the Lake District convinced him "of the excellence of the created universe and of the innate goodness and perfectibility of man." [25] Hence in "The Vale of Esthwaite" (c. 1787), rising in thought above the Gothic and sentimental shards of the poem, Wordsworth looks to the future when memory of the vale, "companion dear / Of childhood's ever merry year," will be a source of sustaining delight. After a melancholy self-reminder that he may soon have to go to work, he concludes the poem affirmatively by saying that, though the "dreary gloom" of "Mammon's joyless mine" may absorb his artistic taste and ability, life "on the mental tablet throws / Each Beauty Art and Nature knows / In tints whose strength tho' time efface / He blends them into softer grace." During his Alpine tour of 1790, Wordsworth writes enthusiastically to Dorothy about the effect nature has had on him; although he has not been intimate with the common Swiss, he thinks that such natural influence would have made them as benevolent as he had found the French to be.[26] In *An Evening Walk,* written during his Cambridge days and published in 1793, Wordsworth can be grateful even for melancholy pains (line 49) while turning his attention to the joys of picturesque nature; and in spite of the dire condition of a wandering wretch and her babes (an episode counterbalanced by the juxtaposed ideal picture of a swan family), Wordsworth ends the poem with a moon-image for hope that smiles on "darling spots" of his past and promises a future of peaceful "golden days." Similar in tone, *Descriptive Sketches* concludes with a vision of liberty lighting the world to another golden age. No doubt this vision derives from the perfectibility inherent to republicanism, a political view which Wordsworth may have learned at Cambridge,[27] but which he certainly learned from Michel Beaupuy in France during 1792.[28] Only the year before, he had commiserated with William

Mathews for his depression of spirits and had written that if the toil and fatigue were removed "you would find that you had been regularly tho' unconsciously advancing. It cannot possibly be otherwise." [29] After the influence of Beaupuy, Wordsworth's optimism burgeoned to encompass national movements, so that he expected "a fairer order of things" to spring from the French Revolution.[30] Even though his hopes for the Revolution flagged when France and England declared war on each other and when the months of Jacobin Terror within France began in mid-1793, by 1795 Wordsworth would have found cause for personal optimism in Raisley Calvert's legacy that enabled him to settle with Dorothy at Racedown and in the succeeding association with both Dorothy and Coleridge. Furthermore, by 1797 Wordsworth and Dorothy could begin to see the favorable results of the natural education they were allowing their ward, young Basil Montagu, Jr.[31]

Despite the fact that Wordsworth tended toward general optimism before 1797, that optimism did not develop into any definite poetic treatment of benevolent necessity. His letter to Mathews quoted above seems to be an exception, but it must be remembered that this is one (perhaps deliberately hyperbolic) statement in an attempt to cheer up Mathews; Mathews' extreme depression may have called for overstated optimism from a close friend. I fail to find any positive idea of unconscious human advance that "cannot possibly be otherwise" in any of Wordsworth's poetry up to 1797. In lines written in 1794 at Windy Brow for a proposed new edition of *An Evening Walk*,[32] Wordsworth shows a new interest in the human mind and man's ability to pierce "the profound of time" and see "whatever man has been and man can be"; but this ability is one granted to, not necessitated upon, man by "Science." However, the animism found in some of these early lines is an advance in Wordsworth's thought as it developed toward a stated belief in benevolent necessity by 1797.

It is probable that in spite of his optimism, Wordsworth did not treat benevolent necessity in his early poetry because he was too much a son of the eighteenth century to rid his muse of the melancholy stances that punctuate many of the early poems, or because in a poem like "Guilt and Sorrow" he was too busy illustrating the deficiencies of the *status quo* in the British constitutional system. Wordsworth could hardly state any consistent faith in benevolent necessity as long as his thought of man could lapse into momentary skepticism like the following in *An Evening Walk*: "Yet still, the sport of some malignant Pow'r, / He knows but from its shade the present hour (lines 41-42)." After these lines were published in 1793, however, Wordsworth ceased to think of man in this way; instead, beginning with the Windy Brow lines of 1794, he pictured man as participating in a sympathy which extends throughout nature.

One thing that prepared him to believe in the ultimate goodness of the world was the characteristic of benevolence in his own family, in himself, and in his friends. The adversity of being orphaned and scattered drew the children closer than ever in their affections for each other.[33] John, who needed little of his share of the children's educational funds, generously wanted the rest of his to go to Wordsworth.[34] Dorothy expressed continued pleasure when the Cooksons (the aunt and uncle with whom she was living) formed a benevolent plan for each day that included the sick and the poor of Forncett.[35] In December 1789 and January 1790 the anti-slavery philanthropist William Wilberforce visited the Cooksons and detected Dorothy's eager benevolence, giving her ten guineas a year to distribute to the poor and presenting her with a copy of Mrs. Sarah Trimmer's *Oeconomy of Charity* (1786), which she read, finding there some hints for improving the condition of the poor by making them the subject of private benevolence.[36] Wordsworth also possessed this benevolent trait. In 1791 he declined William Mathews' tramping venture because it was wrong to put himself in a position to need "those charities of which the acceptance might rob people not half so able to support themselves as myself." [37] Other letters to Mathews are kind attempts to console him for the undesirable conditions under which he has to live and work.[38] Wordsworth's attendance upon Raisley Calvert was charitable in spite of the fact that he came to expect a legacy from the dying man. And though Wordsworth charged Basil Montagu high interest on a loan and received pay for taking Montagu's son as a ward to Racedown, Wordsworth seems to have given Montagu a kind of moral aid that was more valuable than money. In his autobiographical manuscript Montagu wrote of

Wordsworth: "He saw me, with great industry, per-
plexed and misled by passions wild and strong. In the
wreck of my happiness he saw the probable ruin of my
infant. He unremittingly, and to me imperceptibly,
endeavoured to eradicate my faults and to encourage
my good dispositions. I consider having met Wm W. the
most fortunate event in my life." [39] But Wordsworth's
benevolence was not directed solely toward personal
friends as is evidenced by his poem "Guilt and Sorrow,"
of which he said in 1795: "Its object is partly to expose
the vices of the penal law and the calamities of war as
they affect individuals." [40] Some of his friends doubtless
helped stimulate Wordsworth's sense of benevolence.
Robert Jones, the Cambridge friend who accompanied
Wordsworth on his first trip to the Continent in 1790,
made Wordsworth a welcome house guest at Plas-yn-llan
during the following summer and toured Wales on foot
with him; Jones' home was a kind of haven for Wordsworth when he needed one after wandering over Salis-
bury Plain in 1793 and when a lack of means kept him
from London in 1794. John Robinson took Wordsworth's interest to heart by urging him to stay at college
and then by offering him a curacy at Harwich. William
Calvert engaged Wordsworth as his traveling companion
in southern England during the summer of 1793 and
paid the expenses; William and his brother Raisley made
their cottage at Windy Brow available to Wordsworth
and Dorothy in the late winter and spring of 1794; and
at his death in early 1795, Raisley made Wordsworth
economically independent with a legacy of nine hundred

pounds. The Pinney family let Wordsworth and Dorothy use the cottage at Racedown rent-free, beginning in September 1795, and afterwards they helped Wordsworth negotiate with the booksellers. His knowledge of benevolence in his family, in himself, and in his friends would have prepared Wordsworth to recognize benevolence on a larger scale when by 1797 he came to accept universal necessity.

But that part of Wordsworth's general background which united with his optimism to become a belief in benevolent necessity was primarily his experience with nature. Taken chronologically his extant early writing reveals a continuous appreciation for the beauty of natural scenes and for nature's general healthful influence on body, mind, and memory.[41] Five of his early views of nature, though not continuous, are important enough to be isolated here because, since they become vital elements in the *modus operandi* of benevolent necessity, they indicate how well prepared Wordsworth was for developing this mature theme once he accepted its general outlines.

First, the principle (though perhaps not the intricacies) of associationism was known to Wordsworth well before he is supposed to have learned it from Hartley in 1795,[42] the year Wordsworth and Coleridge met. Professor Meyer has found it in the sonnet "Sweet was the walk" of 1792.[43] But it should be noted that the principle applies in the earlier "Vale of Esthwaite" where, for example, Wordsworth mnemonically associates the death of his father with a "naked rock" and a "sharp Hawthorn" and where in the concluding lines he juxtaposes natural details with the value of social affections.

Second, fear, which later figures as an influence equal to natural beauty, is early exemplified in "The Vale of Esthwaite": deliberately turning his back on Gothic elements, Wordsworth presents an acrophobic experience on "the giddy steep," an experience of great, nature-induced fear, heightened by a raging storm. Significantly, he immediately says, "Yet Ah! that soul was never blind / To pleasures of a softer kind," and thereupon describes wild field-flowers and a soft sleeping breeze found in "lovely Grasmere's heavenly vale." Nature, which has some kind of efficacy through man's associative memory, is experienced by man in terms of the polar qualities of beauty and fear.[44]

Third, the monitory quality of natural objects is adumbrated in the "Fragment of a Gothic Tale" when a star above the dungeon roof casts momentary fear into the heart of a youth contemplating murder. Later in Act II of *The Borderers* a similar admonishing star is quite successful in influencing Marmaduke not to kill old Herbert with his own hands.

Fourth, the reciprocal act between man and nature, in which the mind half-creates what it sees, is foreshadowed in the second verse-paragraph of *Descriptive Sketches*. Wordsworth's first definite statement that the senses "half create" is in "Tintern Abbey" (1798), to which he added a note that he was indebted for the idea to Edward Young (*Night Thoughts*, VI, 427); but he had read Young by 1793 and acknowledged a borrowing from him (*Night Thoughts,* V, 1042) in *An Evening Walk* (line 361). According to associational psychology, the original constituent elements of mind are sense impressions, which are compounded into ideas and thought processes. Hence, when in "Tintern Abbey" Wordsworth says that the senses, along with nature, are "The anchor of my purest thoughts," he seems to be utilizing associationism in order to demonstrate that even on the simplest level man's "half creating" of the world around him is really an activity of mind. These lines of 1798 are an early instance of Wordsworth's attempt to fuse or reconcile the opposite concepts of innate ideas and the processes of association upon a *tabula rasa.* Melvin M. Rader pointed to this dualism in Wordsworthian thought [45] in order to correct what he felt was an undue emphasis on Hartleian influence in the study by Arthur Beatty. More important, in fusing the two concepts, Wordsworth has equated the "half creating" senses with mind; and, further, but this give-and-take activity of the mind was early adumbrated in *Descriptive Sketches.* In the second verse-paragraph the poet says that nature gives a "healing pow'r," but only to one like the wanderer who can and will woo her "varying charms." When man is passive ("with heart alive like Memnon's lyre"), he can find "chast'ning thoughts" in every brook; but it is when he is both passive and active ("wooing") that nature is most responsive. The reciprocal process is implied in these lines, but it is noteworthy that at this early date Wordsworth says nothing about it as a *necessary* process.

Fifth, visionary experience was far from new to Wordsworth in 1797. In his earliest poem, written as an exercise at Hawkshead, a vision is the literary framework for the entire poem. The conclusions of both *An Evening Walk* and *Descriptive Sketches* contain optimistic visions of the future. Vision is often attended with a transcendence of the senses that react to nature. Thus in the final lines of "The Dog—An Idyllium" (c. 1786) Wordsworth says that, as he "gaz'd to Nature blind" and a "new-created image" rose in his mind, the result was happiness. In a passage from *Descriptive Sketches* (lines 542-551) the "pastoral Swiss," looking upon the "sainted Rocks" of freedom, feels his spirit soar "beyond the senses and their little reign" to a visionary experience that leads to transcendent communion with God. And in additional lines written for *An Evening Walk* in 1794, Wordsworth, still concerned with sense and vision, writes for the first time of the mind as a mediating agent: the "sober charms" of a rill can "through the mind, by magic influence / Rapt into worlds beyond the reign of sense, / Roll the bright train of neverending dreams." [46]

These, then, constitute Wordsworth's early functional characteristics of nature: associationism, polarity of natural beauty and fear, monition of natural objects, creative reciprocity between man and nature, and visionary experience. If we add to these the oneness of an animistic nature ("secret power," "Nature's impulse") as Wordsworth expressed it in lines added to *An Evening Walk* in 1794,[47] we have the salient features of nature (and man

as part of nature) through which a panentheistic benevolent necessity can operate. With this view of the constitution of nature, his optimistic tendency, and his interest
in benevolence, Wordsworth's thoughts were ideally prepared for a new thematic synthesis. What had been im-
plicit in his poetry now became explicitly stated as the
theme of benevolent necessity. The catalyst that
prompted it was a multiple one discernible through a
brief reconstruction of events which drew Wordsworth's
attention to Hartleian and Godwinian necessity as he
began to write of the progressive powers of nature.

# THREE

# Hartleian and Godwinian Influence

BEFORE THE WINTER of 1797 Wordsworth's thought seems to have been working toward a stated belief in benevolent necessity. For instance, when in 1793 he concluded both *An Evening Walk* and *Descriptive Sketches* with optimistic visions of the future, he seemed to be putting his trust in some force that would direct things toward good. In the lines added to *An Evening Walk* in 1794, the heart that "vibrates evermore" with "feeling" universal sympathy (because of a "secret power" found in all forms of nature) is a heart that has accepted the idea of animism; although the lines do not state that everything works inevitably toward good, the heart that sympathizes with all natural forms and "their social accents never vainly hears" may be a heart that, by implication at least, has discovered and accepted the determinism of benevolent necessity. In *The Borderers* Wordsworth is concerned with the problem of determinism, but the action of the play does not indicate that he has made up his mind about it. The villain Oswald says that the smallest accident might change the course of major events, but all of his arguments in the play are either specious or opportunistic, variable according to their efficacy in misleading Marmaduke into committing murder. There is the benevolent star that shines through a crevice in the dungeon and stops Marmaduke from slaying blind old Herbert with his hands, but the star serves only the dramatic purpose of delaying action: Marmaduke later deserts Herbert on the moor, deliberately leaving him—defenseless and without food—to be judged by God. Though Herbert is innocent of all wrongdoing, he dies on the moor, and his death is not stressed as a link in a development toward a greater good. The only suggestion in the play that evil may be subordinate to good comes near the end when Marmaduke, now aware of how Oswald has duped him into being the cause of Herbert's death, accepts a life of remorse and urges the same upon Oswald.

> When seas and continents shall lie between us—
> The wider space the better—we may find
> In such a course fit links of sympathy,
> An incommunicable rivalship
> Maintained, for peaceful ends beyond our view.
> (V, 2274-2278)

The idea in this last line, however, is not connected directly with Herbert's death. If Wordsworth intended for the play to illustrate the theme of benevolent necessity, he might have made more of this idea, of elements like the benevolent star, and of the kind of good effect that Herbert says he and his daughter Idonea had on people when the two of them were wandering the country in a destitute condition—a good effect quite similar to that which was wrought by the old Cumberland beggar within the context of benevolent necessity. Wordsworth may have had something like benevolent necessity in mind as he wrote *The Borderers*; but perhaps because he did not make any character in the play his *raisonneur*, he left his treatment of the theme inconclusive. Nonetheless, the drama makes clear that the idea of necessity was on his mind as he was writing, and this same concern may lie behind statements in "Lines Left upon a Seat in a Yew-tree," a poem that he completed in the same year of 1797. He tells a traveler that the "curling waves" of the lake "shall lull thy mind / By one soft impulse saved from vacancy." Even the man of pride is sometimes subdued by nature to feel benevolence, but the greatest benevolence is that which comprehends the oneness of the created universe: "he who feels contempt / For any living thing, hath faculties / Which he has never used."

Thus, between 1794 and 1797 Wordsworth seems to have been concerned with the idea of benevolent necessity, but it was not until the winter of 1797 that he actually stated the theme and began a consistent development of it in his poetry. How and why did he bring the theme into clarified prominence by the end of that year? The answer seems to lie in a convergence of circumstances recently revaluated in part, with new evidence at hand, by David V. Erdman.[1] The clearest interpretation of the circumstances is that, when the right catalyst came, Wordsworth had been prepared for a new thematic synthesis by three primary conditions: his personal experience with "natural" education; the influence of David Hartley's writings, buttressed by Coleridge's high respect for the associationist; and the similar influence of William Godwin's philosophy—this also supported by Coleridge's enthusiasm. Most aspects of the first two conditions have become generally accepted facts by critics and may be synopsized. The third condition, having been long debated, now seems susceptible to proof because of new evidence and the consequent reëxamination of Wordsworth's so-called anti-Godwinian poems. This proof merits more extended and detailed presentation. It may well be, however, that these three conditions would not have coalesced at this time into a conviction about benevolent necessity had it not been for the catalytic proposal of the philanthropic Wedgwood brothers.

Tom Wedgwood, eager to devote money and time to his own and his brother Josiah's philosophic ideas about education, visited Wordsworth at Alfoxden for a period of five days (15-20 September 1797) in order to sound him out as a candidate for superintendent of a nursery of genius. Both Wordsworth and Coleridge were being considered as superintendents. But judging from the plans that Wedgwood put forth in a letter to William Godwin earlier in July,[2] Wordsworth reacted against the man-made restrictive methods of the proposed nursery and began to examine the disciplinary system that nature had employed in educating him. In addition to his own experience, he had before him more recent evidence of nature's teaching: the highly promising effects of two years of "natural" education on young Basil Montagu, Jr.[3]

Wordsworth's immediate response to the Wedgwood proposal was the thinly-veiled autobiographical treatment of the Pedlar that he added to "The Ruined Cottage," lines composed during the winter of 1797-1798.[4] But these additional lines (as well as the poem "The Old Cumberland Beggar," begun in late 1797) contain a statement that goes beyond the idea of nature's merely disciplinary education. Lying behind the interaction of sympathy between man and all other things is a moral determinism:

> Thus deeply drinking in the soul of things
> We shall be wise perforce, and we shall move
> From strict necessity along the path
> Of order and of good.
> (*Poetical Works*, V, 402-403)

Derived as it doubtless was from Wordsworth's intercourse with nature, this concise idea of a benevolent necessity appears to have been strengthened by the works of Hartley and Godwin. Probably these works helped him to formulate the poetic expression of his belief.

The evidence for Hartley's influence may be summarized briefly. As early as 1829 Harriet Martineau recognized the links between Hartley and Wordsworth,[5] but the prominence of Hartleian psychology in Words-

worth's poetry was first convincingly demonstrated in
1922 by Arthur Beatty. Yet the date when this influence
began is debatable. Wordsworth's poetry illustrates associationism prior to 1795,[6] the date suggested by Beatty,
and it is possible (though not provable) that Wordsworth knew Priestley's abridged second edition of Hartley's *Observations on Man, His Frame, His Duty, and
His Expectations* (1749) which his own publisher, Joseph Johnson, had printed in 1790.[7] On the other hand,
in 1791 Johnson published a three-volume edition and a
one-volume edition of Hartley's *Observations*, both editions containing the notes of Hartley's German trans-
lator, Hermann Andreas Pistorius.[8] The three-volume
edition—the one used for this comparative study—is the
one Coleridge had read and referred to in notes to "Religious Musings," and it may have been the one with
which Wordsworth was conversant.

It was not until late 1797, however, after the Wedgwood proposal turned Wordsworth's thoughts to the education fostered by nature, that Wordsworth definitely
expressed the theme of benevolent necessity. That expression and its correspondence with Hartley's views
may have owed much to the stimulation of Coleridge,
with whom Wordsworth established a real intimacy beginning in 1797.

Coleridge, having moved to Nether Stowey by 1 January, was within some thirty miles of Racedown; in
July the Wordsworths moved from Racedown to Alfoxden only three miles away from Coleridge. Coleridge
may have already introduced Wordsworth to the writ-

ings of Hartley as early as 1795 when the two poets first
met, for Coleridge had twice given Hartley footnote
credit for ideas in "Religious Musings" of 1794-1796,[9]
and he continued to utilize Hartleian ideas in subsequent
poems. The belief that all things work purposively for
good is found in the conclusion of "The Destiny of Na-
tions," in "Ver Perpetuum" and an accompanying footnote, and in the introduction of "Ode to the Departing
Year"—all compositions of 1796. Two years later, at the
height of Wordsworth and Coleridge's relationship,
Coleridge wrote "The Rime of the Ancient Mariner,"
which illustrates benevolent necessity: the Mariner is
compelled to relate his story to people like the Wedding-
Guest who "cannot choose but hear"; the purpose of
such frame-racking compulsion is to spread knowledge
of the oneness of the world and sympathy for all creatures in the world.[10] Certainly, beginning in 1797,
Coleridge had opportunity to reinforce Wordsworth's
knowledge of Hartley, the associationist who had ana-
lyzed the concept of necessity and had emphasized its
importance.

It is true that Coleridge could also have discussed William Godwin's *Enquiry Concerning Political Justice* with
equal discernment and possibly some of the enthusiasm
of his 1795 sonnet on the subject. But in this case Wordsworth would have contributed at least as much to the
discussion as did Coleridge. Wordsworth was already
well acquainted with Godwin personally, and Professor
Meyer is doubtless correct in his belief that Godwin sent
Wordsworth to the writings of Hartley and Hartley in

turn sent Wordsworth enthusiastically back to Godwin's *Political Justice*.[11] Quite probably his knowledge
of Godwin and Hartley made Wordsworth more influential on Coleridge than *vice versa, The Borderers* making an impress on the latter's *Osorio,* and "Lines Left
upon a Seat in a Yew-tree" perhaps contributing to
the concept about the oneness of the world as Coleridge
expressed it later in "The Rime of the Ancient Mariner."
The stimulation by Coleridge suggested here, then, is not
that which redirects someone's thinking but rather that
which comes from being an interested listener who also
contributes much to a discussion.

Since it is often difficult, if not impossible, to determine whether Godwin or Hartley is the primary influence on certain Wordsworthian ideas (particularly the
theme of benevolent necessity), it seems profitable to
marshal evidence that Wordsworth in 1797 was in a
frame of mind to accept the Godwinian concept of necessity that agreed with Hartley's. This evidence is three-
fold: (1) Wordsworth's personal acquaintance with
Godwin, (2) Godwin's significant modifications concerning rationality and emotion in the second and third
editions of *Political Justice,* and (3) a revaluation of
some of Wordsworth's so-called anti-Godwinian poetry.

The new evidence of Wordsworth's acquaintance with
Godwin comes from the Godwin diary in Duke University's Abinger Collection, presently being edited by Professor Lewis Patton.[12] Wordsworth met Godwin at a tea
on 27 February 1795 and called upon him the very next
day. From that time until Wordsworth's removal from

London to Racedown in the autumn, the two men called upon each other nine more times. Considering that Godwin was a busy man—among other things, preparing the second edition of *Political Justice*—and was out of town during part of June and July, the frequent interchange of visits suggests the probability of mutual agreement and influence. Such an inference is bolstered by the fact that, although Wordsworth was happily sequestered at Racedown during 1796, in June he and Godwin met four times before the latter left London on 1 July. Again on 13 December 1797 Wordsworth called upon Godwin; this visit was during the winter when Wordsworth first emphasized benevolent necessity in his poetry. Although we have no evidence of immediate subsequent visits, the two men called, met, and corresponded with something like regularity from 1806 until 1835, the year before Godwin's death.

Another bit of *ana* seems important in relation to this argument, for it may well relate to Wordsworth's early acquaintance with Godwin. In *The Plain Speaker* (May 1826) William Hazlitt bluntly disparaged Godwin's conversational abilities, saying that Godwin reserved his stores of understanding and genius for books rather than for conversation and that what little he said was both dull and nonsensical. In the Abinger Collection is the draft of a reply in which Godwin attempted to refute Hazlitt's slur with evidence. Among the prominent men drawn to his conversational ability, according to Godwin, was Wordsworth. "I had the honour, in the talk of one evening, to convert Wordsworth from the doctrine of self-love to that of benevolence—ask him." [13] In light of Wordsworth's early benevolent tendency noted in Chapter II, it is probable that Wordsworth and Godwin simply *agreed* that benevolence was better than self-love. If there was any conversation, it doubtless involved merely Wordsworth's approval of the philosophic framework that Godwin's interests would have given to benevolence. When this conversion took place may never be known, but it seems reasonable to believe that it occurred during the early acquaintance when the poet and political philosopher would most likely be expounding ideas and learning from each other.

Godwin's close association of benevolence and necessity within the moral context of his philosophy was parallel to much of Wordsworth's thinking. To Godwin benevolent intention is essential to moral virtue,[14] and habit, which is partly the result of inevitable conditioning by outside influences, can transmute self-love into benevolence.[15] Morality, says Godwin, will never "show like itself, till man shall be acknowledged for what he really is, a being capable of rectitude, virtue and benevolence." [16] Like benevolence, necessity too is integral to morality; in fact, Godwin specifically calls it the "doctrine of moral necessity" [17] and states that "the idea of moral discipline proceeds entirely upon this principle" of necessity.[18] His definition of necessity [19] is mechanistic: since the process of cause and effect is universally applicable, a person's acts, whether voluntary (that is, volitional) or involuntary (that is, instinctive or habitual), are predetermined by numerous causes; very often even voluntary acts become matters of habit. All are necessary acts, however; and since man is perfectible,[20] since necessity teaches "that all things in the universe are connected together," [21] and since in the universe is a "general tendency to improvement," [22] it follows that all things ultimately partake of a necessary moral perfectibility (as distinguished from perfection). Godwin cannot avoid some involuted argument, but it should be clear that morality is his basic criterion for benevolence and necessity as well as for the subject of politics in general.

Morality is also a basic criterion for Wordsworth. For instance, in the Prospectus (spring 1798) for *The Recluse* he writes of "moral strength" and hopes that his song will shine with "star-like virtue," shedding "benignant influence." In the 1800 Preface to *Lyrical Ballads* his stated purpose is a moral one: ". . . if the views with which they [the poems] were composed were indeed realised, a class of Poetry would be produced . . . not unimportant in the quality, and in the multiplicity of its moral relations." [23] Since morality is pervasive in Wordsworth's writing, it is no surprise to find it basic to Wordsworthian necessity. In the 1797-1798 lines on the character of the Pedlar (the lines containing "strict necessity" quoted above), Wordsworth, like Godwin, links together in a moral framework ideas about habit, interrelationship, benevolence, and necessity. Once a man is taught to love "such objects as excite / No morbid passions no disquietude / No vengeance, and no hatred," he feels the "pure principle of love" and he "cannot

choose / But seek for objects of a kindred love / In fel-
low-natures . . .": "He seeks for good and finds the good
he seeks." When we are disciplined by such objects, by
science in proper perspective, and by natural imagery,
"all things shall live in us and we shall live / In all things
that surround us." Because of interrelational influences,
we acquire the "habit by which sense is made / Subservient still to moral purposes," and we find in "general
laws / And local accidents" that a "chain of good / Shall
link us to our kind." [24] Allowing for Godwin's political
bias and for Wordsworth's inclusion of the function of
nature, there is still much similarity between the two
men's attitudes towards benevolence and necessity: both
are founded in morality. Significantly, however, Godwin's written expression of benevolent necessity preceded that of Wordsworth and is therefore likely to have
influenced the latter. If, as Godwin said, he "converted"
Wordsworth to benevolence, Wordsworth may well have
found himself agreeing with Godwin's philosophic moral
framework, which relied heavily on the doctrine of necessity—so heavily, in fact, that on page 363 in Volume
I of *Political Justice*, the point at which he begins to examine necessity in detail, Godwin indicates that the
"principle" of necessity is integral to all the preceding
argument of his book.

Nonetheless, a question arises. Why did not Wordsworth state the theme sooner after the first edition of *Political Justice* in 1793 or shortly after his initial acquaintance with Godwin in 1795? First of all, it is known only
that Wordsworth had read the first edition sometime

before he made his earliest extant reference to it in a letter of 21 March 1796.[25] Second, it is well to remember that in the Preface to *Lyrical Ballads* Wordsworth says that poetry comes from recollection; only after feelings and ideas have been absorbed to the point of tranquility can they give rise to "the spontaneous overflow of powerful feelings" that constitute poetry; a passage of time is requisite. Third, prior to 1797 there seems to have been no catalytic circumstance quite like the rejected Wedgwood offer and the reciprocal discussions with Coleridge that would have focused Wordsworth's attention more closely than before on the determining influence of nature and on the related philosophic views of Hartley and Godwin. Yet Godwin may have been a factor in the Wedgwood affair, for though Wordsworth might have found sanction elsewhere as well, he could have found it in Godwin, not only for the kind of education he was giving young Montagu but also for his rejection of the Wedgwood methods. With no essential changes from the 1793 to the 1798 editions, Godwin gave the following dicta about a child's right to individuality in his educative process:

No man will think of vexing with premature learning the feeble and inexperienced, lest, when they came [sic] to years of discretion, they should refuse to be learned. The mind will be suffered to expand itself, in proportion as occasion and impression shall excite it, and not tortured and enervated by being cast in a particular mould. No creature in human form will be expected to learn any thing, but because he desires it, and has some conception of its value; and every man, in proportion to his capacity, will be ready to furnish such general hints and comprehensive views, as will suffice for the guidance and encouragement of him who studies from the impulse of desire.[26]

Judging from this attitude toward education, one can imagine that Godwin would have reacted to the Wedgwood proposal about as Wordsworth did.

There is, however, another aspect of Godwinian thought that is crucial: Godwin's attempt by the time of his second edition (and his final success with the 1797 revisions for the third edition) to place feelings on as important a level as rationality in his treatment of human morals and happiness.

Since the dates and frequency of Wordsworth's and Godwin's interchange of visits suggest mutual agreement and influence, in their reciprocity of influence doubtless lies the crux and perhaps the answer to a problem that has taxed much scholarly thought—Wordsworth's supposed reaction against Godwinian rationalism. The problem, I think, has been too simply stated in terms of antithesis (Wordsworthian emotion as opposed to Godwinian reason), with Wordsworth rejecting rationalism for feeling.[27] Sometimes this oversimplification can lead to hasty critical reading of Wordsworth. In a notebook that contains manuscript JJ of *The Prelude* and dates from the winter of 1798-1799 when Wordsworth and his sister were in Gosler, Germany, is "a fragment of a moral essay exposing the weakness of 'systems' such as Godwin's."[28] Although F. W. Bateson[29] refers to this essay while arguing that Wordsworth was never a disciple of Godwin and consequently never reacted against him, the essay actually utilizes Godwinian terms and criteria (for example, habits, benevolence) and nowhere argues against the content of a system like Godwin's. Indeed, though Wordsworth reacts against philosophic reasoning that fails to reach a reader emotionally, he says nothing against reason as a philosophic concept. In criticising Godwin's procedure rather than his thought, Wordsworth's essay simply argues the supremacy of poetic writing over "scientific" writing.[30]

It is not surprising to find that Wordsworth does not reject reason in his essay, for what he actually does in earlier works like *The Borderers* and "Lines Left upon a Seat in a Yew-tree" is to show, not that rationalism *per se* is bad, but that reason and intellectual pride can be bad when they are excessive.[31] Furthermore, it should be noted that in both of these works rationalism is not divorced from emotion: Oswald's perverted rationalism stems from his earlier emotional reaction when he committed an unintentional wrong in slaying his ship's captain only to learn afterwards that the captain was innocent; the man in "The Yew-tree Lines" is remarkable for his emotion of pride more than for any demonstrated intellect, and he reacts with the emotion of continued solitary resentment when society fails to recognize his intellectual powers. For those who argue that the latter poem is anti-Godwinian, one may note that the subject of the poem is benevolence,[32] that even the man of intellect is moved to emotional sighs and tears at the thought of benevolent persons (in one manuscript version they are called "those kindred beings"), and that in Godwinian tradition Wordsworth subtly blames society for the man's morbid reaction to the world's inimical neglect of him—since society does absolutely nothing, positive or negative, by default society is to blame. One may remember also that a primary theme of the poem is participation versus the isolation of solitude, a theme that Wordsworth later develops in *The Excursion* through the Wanderer's advice to and exhortation of the Solitary. Godwin too had set up strictures against solitude; and although he preferred persuasive representation over exhortation, he felt that man was obligated to assist others with corrective censure.[33] But reality, as Godwin saw, was in sharp contrast with his ideals, for in his novels he continued what B. Sprague Allen has called "Godwin's characteristic portrayal of the tragic isolation of the individual deprived of communion with his fellows." [34] Certainly the thematic similarities between Godwin's writings and Wordsworth's poem are remarkable.

Rather than simply rejecting Godwinian reason, in *The Borderers* and "The Yew-tree Lines" Wordsworth, like Godwin, is tempering reason with feeling and illustrating the intricate relationship of the two human characteristics. In 1795, when Wordsworth and Coleridge first met and read their latest poetry to each other, it was this very "union of deep feeling with profound thought" that impressed Coleridge with "Guilt and Sorrow." [35] In the 1800 Preface to *Lyrical Ballads*—and particularly in the 1802 additions to the Preface—the words *thought* and *feeling* (or their equivalents) seldom occur except in conjunction, whether Wordsworth discusses what constitutes the poet, the reader, or man as poetic subject matter; furthermore, the moral essence of poetry—in terms of content, purpose, and effect—includes both rationalism and emotion, one stemming from the other or both active at once. The 1802 Appendix states that the truth of emotion in poetic diction is decided by judgment and understanding. If at times *thought, judgment,* and *understanding* seem equivalent to *taste,* we may remember that in the 1815 "Essay, Supplementary to the Preface" Wordsworth writes that taste, like imagination, is a matter of "intellectual *acts* and *operations*" (Wordsworth's italics). There can be little doubt, I think, that Wordsworth meant to keep rationalism and emotion in relative equipoise.

Godwin, on the other hand, increasingly acknowledged the value of emotion after the 1793 edition of *Political Justice* and thus modified his own emphasis on reason. Professors Basil Willey and F. E. L. Priestley [36] have noted Godwin's changing attitude toward human emotion, but it was not part of their studies to relate that change to Wordsworth's acceptance of benevolent necessity. In a very discerning article B. Sprague Allen [37] demonstrated that from the time of *Caleb Williams* (1794) Godwin developed in his novels the idea that feeling is a prime motive for conduct, an idea that germinated from some of the principles of *Political Justice*; but Mr. Allen seems not to have detected the elevation

of feeling in subsequent editions of *Political Justice,* and
he does not connect Godwin's changed attitude with
Wordsworth's belief in feeling, doubtless because he follows the tradition that the purpose of *The Borderers* was
"to expose Godwinian fallacies." Yet in the year that
*The Borderers* was completed, 1797, Godwin was writing in *The Enquirer* that "man has not only an understanding to reason, but a heart to feel." [38] Godwin's
changing attitude toward emotion is so highly significant
that it would be remiss not to trace its development and
its relation to Wordsworth.

Thus, in 1793, although he says that it would be dis-
graceful of those qualified as public instructors should
"they stain their benignity, by showing that that benignity has not become the inmate of their hearts," [39] Godwin does not admit the validity of feeling or passion as
a psychological entity. While he does admit "desire" as a
motivation in education, he denies the "independent operations of reason and passion" and gives a definition of *passion* that corresponds obversely with Wordsworth's
definition of *thoughts* in the 1800 Preface as "the repre-
sentatives of all our past feelings": the word *passion,*
"which has produced such extensive mischief in the philosophy of mind," signifies only vivid thoughts.[40] This is
the general extent of Godwin's 1793 view of passion or
feeling; and it must have been a reliance on Godwin's
early view only, or possibly a reliance on a reading of
Leslie Stephen's comments,[41] that led Emile Legouis to
say that "Godwin has endeavoured to make all the feelings subservient to the intelligence, and has asserted that

the only justification for affection lies in its subordination to the law of general utility." [42] Godwin's early attitude, however, was soon to undergo some radical readjusting.

In October 1795—eight months after he and Wordsworth first met and subsequently called upon each other ten more times—Godwin wrote a new preface about the changes he had made for the 1796 edition of *Political Justice*. Among these changes is a significant one in a newly added chapter: he says that "without doubt passion cannot be eradicated," that

> passion is so far from being incompatible with reason, that it is inseparable from it. Virtue, sincerity, justice, and all those principles which are begotten and cherished in us by a due exercise of reason, will never be very strenuously espoused, till they are ardently loved . . . In this sense nothing is necessary, but to show us that a thing is truly good and worthy to be desired, in order to excite in us a passion for its attainment.[43]

Godwin is no longer saying that *passion* is only a misnomer for a kind of thought or rationality; rather, passion or feeling stands in direct, intricate relationship with rationality: "Sublime and expansive ideas produce delicious emotions" [44] which are important to the permanence of knowledge and virtue.[45] Godwin can go so far as to replace a chapter that emphasized utility [46] with one entitled "Of Good and Evil" in which he says, "The pleasures of the mere man of taste and refinement, 'play round the head, but come not to the heart.' " By slightly

misquoting from Pope's "An Essay on Man" (IV, 254),
Godwin elevates the man of benevolence above the man
of refinement; the one most worthy of emulation is a
man of feeling. This is strange language for a man who is
supposed to have emphasized rationality so exclusively
that Wordsworth reacted strenuously against it.

In reality Wordsworth and Godwin were in remarkable general agreement on the relationship of emotion
and rationality in the constitution of man. In July of
1797, the year when Wordsworth completed *The Borderers* and "The Yew-tree Lines" as we know the poem,
Godwin had finished the revisions and additions for his
1798 edition of *Political Justice* and had given feeling a
prime importance. In the new "Summary of Principles"
he stressed the "pleasures of intellectual feeling" [47] and
added this: "The voluntary actions of men are under the
direction of their feelings. Reason is not an independent
principle, and has no tendency to excite us to action; in
a practical view, it is merely a comparison and balancing
of different feelings." [48] Formerly, in defining voluntary
action, Godwin had said that the motive to action was
the "idea of certain consequences"; but now the "idea"
has been replaced with an emotion, the "hope or fear of
that event." [49] "In subjects connected with the happiness
of mankind," he says, "the feeling is the essence." [50] In
his argument against punishment, Godwin calls for reformation that relies equally on feeling *and* rationality:
"Reformation is improvement; and nothing can take
place in a man worthy the name of improvement, otherwise than by an appeal to the unbiassed judgment of his

mind, and the essential feelings of his nature." [51] Clearly, in 1797 Wordsworth and Godwin were both emphasizing emotion as well as rationality, and it may well be that Wordsworth was now influencing Godwin to acknowledge the importance of emotion. Since there was no battle line between them on this issue of the constitution of human nature, it seems highly probable that Wordsworth would have heeded the content of Godwin's moral thought that stressed benevolent necessity.

The problem of feelings-versus-rationalism, however, is not the only one that merits reëxamination in reference to the reciprocal influence of Godwin and Wordsworth. Because in *The Prelude* Wordsworth relates how he reacted to rationalism and "yielded up moral questions in despair," [52] some critics have decided that the reaction was specifically to Godwin and that the moral crisis probably came in 1795 and 1796.[53] But biographical evidence has been convincingly advanced to prove that from 1794 to 1797 Wordsworth's mind was not wasting under any disease-like crisis.[54] In spite of such evidence, however, some dubious ideas about Wordsworth's "anti-Godwinian" poetry persist and call for reëxamination.

Some simple correspondences between the views of Godwin and Wordsworth may first be cited. For example, as others have noted, both express a critical attitude toward war and its consequences. They indicate a need for penal reform. Each puts some emphasis on stoicism.[55] The moral purpose in Wordsworth's 1800 Preface relies heavily on the psychological principle of pleasure, while the same principle is inherent to Godwin's concept of justice and morality.[56] For Godwin a belief in necessity leads to tranquility, particularly for a man who has had the emotion of benevolence.[57] In the Preface Wordsworth says that poetry "takes its origin from emotion recollected in tranquillity." Godwin's saying that a cheerful mind (particularly when the source of cheerfulness is benevolence) is an aid to convalescence [58] brings to mind Wordsworth's "The Idiot Boy," in which the old and critically ill Susan Gale becomes well again because of her selfless concern and search for the strayed idiot, Johnny Foy. In addition to all of these simple correspondences between Godwinian and Wordsworthian ideas and attitudes, one of more complexity should be mentioned: Wordsworth's turning, according to the Preface, to humble and rustic life for poetic diction and subject matter perhaps owes much to Godwin's praise of simple, natural society (particularly the reference to the "real nature" of man living in a small parish where government would be mostly a matter of individual self-restraint); genuine political justice, Godwin felt, would result in this kind of ideal society.[59]

Since "Lines Left upon a Seat in a Yew-tree," shows that Wordsworth, like Godwin, prefers participation to the isolation of solitude, the premise follows that both value dynamic rather than static existence. Godwin's discussion of linguistic improvement (which he parallels with moral improvement)[60] and his praise for the advance of "modern literature" as he reacts against the static quality of eighteenth-century optimism [61] remind

one that in the 1800 Preface and 1802 Appendix Wordsworth reacted strongly against the static quality of
eighteenth-century poetic diction. But Wordsworth
would have found further discussion congenial to him
in Godwin's strictures against what he saw as eighteenth-century inflexibility. Because of Lord Lonsdale's
successful legal maneuvers in refusing to discharge his
obligation of forty-seven hundred pounds to the estate
of Wordsworth's deceased father,[62] Wordsworth, in sore
need of funds, acknowledged the grim truth in Godwin's
criticism against the purchasing of legal victory by the
dictatorial and tyrannical rich; [63] and he would have
agreed with Godwin that litigation in a free state is endless and that law is bad because it tries to make things
static rather than to allow them to be progressive.[64] In
fact, Wordsworth may well have had Godwin's chapter
on law in mind when, according to Hazlitt, he told the
student at the Temple to study Godwin on necessity.
Certainly Wordsworth's personal experience with eighteenth-century literature and law puts him on the side of
Godwin in emphasizing dynamic progress.

So far, most of the parallelism between Godwin's and
Wordsworth's ideas just discussed has gone either un-
contested or unnoted by critics, but critics have investi-
gated one subject, property, and have denied that the
two men's ideas were parallel.[65] The subject deserves further scrutiny. Because of a reaction against Godwinian
rationality, Wordsworth is believed to have chosen the
love of property as a poetic subject that would confute
Godwin's reasonings against property. But the poet and

the philosopher were not at odds about rationality and emotion, and I contend as well that they were not really opposed on the subject of property.

Unlike some of his critics, Wordsworth, eclectic in developing his themes, was more interested in writing of experience than in writing rebuttals. The love of property in "Michael" (1800) is often looked upon as defiance of Godwin's strictures against such love.[66] But Godwin's doctrine of property is this: "Every man has a right to that, the exclusive possession of which being awarded to him, a greater sum of benefit or pleasure will result, than could have arisen from its being otherwise appropriated." [67] This utilitarian view is quite applicable to Michael's land, which "with a few sheep, with rocks and stones, and kites" is "an utter solitude," a land of hardship that few others could have desired. No one else could have worked harder day and night than Michael and his family in "the certainty of honourable gains"; and no one else could have equaled Michael's "pleasurable feeling of blind love" that came in associative memory from the objects of the hereditary landscape around him. Furthermore, of Godwin's three degrees of property (1. the means of subsistence and happiness; 2. one's empire over the produce of his own industry; and 3. the labor of others [68]) the first two apply equally to Michael's situation. Inheritance that usurps the labor of others is bad, but under present economic conditions (here as elsewhere Godwin is against abrupt revolution) the rights of the second degree of property may mitigate such inherited "usurpation" so long as the inheritance does not

create luxury that disallows to others the means of subsistence and happiness. It is the first degree of property,
however, that is most applicable to Michael, who needs
the land and also has the right to his own produce of
industry which entails no usurpation of the labor of others. Michael's love of the land comes within Godwin's
"greater sum of . . . pleasure," for no stranger could vie
with Michael because of the latter's long associations and
consanguinity with the land; and none could probably
gain greater beneficial subsistence from it even by enclosure. The prohibitive cost of enclosure, as both
Godwin and Wordsworth must have known from eighteenth-century practices, would have forced someone
like Michael from his land, driving him into penury
while adding to the profits of a large landlord.

"Michael," then, is hardly a poem designed to refute
Godwin on property. Moreover, only two years earlier
(and hence closer in time to Wordsworth's so-called "rejection" of Godwin) the poem "The Last of the Flock"
(1798) presents a man whose love of property (his
sheep) exceeds his love for his own family and drives
him to contemplate wicked deeds when he is refused
parish relief because he still has such property. It is impossible to believe that Wordsworth is here extolling the
love of property when that love leads a man to evil and
to negligence of his own needy family. In "Goody Blake
and Harry Gill" (also of 1798) Wordsworth offers a
pointed lesson on the excessive love of property, a lesson
that Godwin would have applauded: because he refuses
to let old and frail Goody Blake gather sticks from his

hedge in order to keep herself warm, Harry Gill suffers the curse of being perpetually cold and chattering. In "Beggars" (1802) Wordsworth again seems to be critical of undue love of property, in this instance a love that causes beggar-children to lie for money. The evidence of these poems indicates that Wordsworth could be as critical of property as was Godwin and that his attitude toward property at times could be based on the same utilitarian principles of pleasure and benefit as was Godwin's attitude. Instead of deciding from a number of selected poems that Wordsworth has taken a stand for or against the ideas of another writer, critics are perhaps more justified in assuming that, when a writer's idea coincided with the poet's own experience and poetic purpose, Wordsworth did not hesitate to utilize the idea in terms of actual belief—or, for that matter, in terms of mythic belief, as in his use of the Platonic concept of immortality in the "Intimations Ode." Judging therefore from the evidence in Wordsworth's and Godwin's writings, one may safely say that Wordsworth did not bother himself at all with refuting Godwin's ideas on property.

A final subject calling for clarification in the Wordsworth's-rejection-of-Godwin problem is that of lying. Of "Anecdote for Fathers" (1798) Legouis says this:

> To one who had learnt from Godwin that lying is opposed to human nature, and would never have existed but for the indirect compulsion of societies and religions, it must have been a revelation to hear a child tell a bold and harmless lie, without any apparent motive . . .[69]

It seems to me that the point of the anecdote is not just the "feelings of wonder at the instincts and emotions" of a child, but more a realization about "the indirect compulsion" of adult society that gives a child an obvious motive to lie. Five times Wordsworth urges the boy to tell him why he prefers Kilve to the present Liswyn farm, thus forcing the boy to give a reason that is untrue. In the original version of the poem Wordsworth, a member of supposedly discerning adult society, says, "I talked to him / In very idleness." This statement, coupled with the original subtitle ("Shewing how the art of lying may be taught"), points obviously to the hundredfold lesson that Wordsworth says he learned from the boy: that idle, unreasoning questions violate the boy's love of place by teaching him to lie. Such a lesson, critical of unreason and of the inadvertent teaching of lying, is quite Godwinian.

The evidence adduced here indicates that Wordsworth's and Godwin's ideas were in greater general agreement than most critics have hitherto admitted. The poet and the philosopher were intimately acquainted before and during the time that Wordsworth began writing of benevolent necessity in his poetry of 1797. Godwin's elevation of emotion (perhaps a result of Wordsworth's influence) as a psychological entity in *Political Justice* after 1793 would have made the content of his thought concerning necessity acceptable to Wordsworth. And as a revaluation of Wordsworth's so-called anti-Godwinian poetry illustrates, the two writers were not at odds about property and lying any more than they were about war, progress, and legal injustice.

By 1797, then, Wordsworth was well acquainted with the works of Godwin and Hartley and was in agreement with them. His interest in them was bolstered by the enthusiasm of Coleridge. His personal experience with "natural" education, he now found upon reëxamination, had been a matter of meliorative "strict necessity" all along. Consequently, the coalescent circumstances were exactly right for him to utilize Godwinian ideas that would send him also to Hartleian ideas as he reacted to the Wedgwood proposal and developed his theme of benevolent necessity in his poetry of the Great Decade.

# FOUR

# Oneness and Interrelationships

WORDSWORTH'S THEME OF benevolent necessity is a
major one, but it is not the only theme during the Great
Decade, and it often enough dovetails with others, sometimes supporting and sometimes being supported by
them. Like any other man's, Wordsworth's thoughts are
fashioned of many parts; but if those thoughts are consistent unto themselves within a given period of time,
then there must be an interpretive synthesis that pre-
cludes the contradiction of one thought or theme by another. In a recent study David Perkins emphasizes
Wordsworth's sense of a cleavage or chasm between the
world of nature and the world of man.[1] Professor
Perkins' thesis is that in a poem like "Nutting" (1798)
and in several of the spots-of-time episodes in *The Prelude* Wordsworth feels something inimical and alien in
nature. An equally valid interpretation—and the one
adopted here—is that these experiences with nature il-

lustrate the "ministry of fear," [2] one example of the *modus operandi* of benevolent necessity working through natural monition. In tracing the course of events that gave direction to his own life, Wordsworth says in *The Prelude* (I, 305-306) that "fair seed-time had my soul, and I grew up / Foster'd alike by beauty and by fear." During the Great Decade Wordsworth's illustrations of fearful natural events appear to point less to a sense of the cleavage between man and nature than to a realization of the "goadings on," the "severer interventions," the "ministry" of a progressive force whose purpose is "to impregnate and to elevate the mind." [3]

Relying heavily on symbolic interpretation that can ferret out meanings apparently hidden to the conscious thought of a writer, Professor Perkins reads "Nutting" as a poem with sexual symbolism for man's violation of nature, a violation that points to the chasm between man and nature.[4] One cannot deny that a kind of rapacity is enacted by the youth who came upon "one dear nook / Unvisited," who viewed the hazels "with tempting clusters hung" and then dallied like a lover before ravaging "both branch and bough," which, along with the rest of the nook, "patiently gave up / Their quiet being." Whether consciously meant or not, however, sexual ravishment is a kind of union (note the patient giving up), not a separation; and one can gain a lesson from the "sense of pain" that comes from viewing the scene of ravagement. The lesson is formulated when, in concluding the poem, Wordsworth turns to his sister and cautions her to "move along these shades / In gentleness of heart; with gentle hand / Touch—for there is a spirit in the woods." Elsewhere Wordsworth writes often of a union between man and this natural spirit of the universe—so often that it can be called wedding imagery. In the Prospectus to *The Excursion,* lines written perhaps as early as spring 1798 and intended as an indication of the design and scope of his major lengthy work (that is, *The Prelude, The Excursion,* and *The Recluse*), Wordsworth envisions the time when the "discerning intellect of Man" will be "wedded to this goodly universe / In love and holy passion," and he proceeds to "chant" "the spousal verse / Of this great consummation" (lines 52-58). Unless one intentionally isolates a symbol and thereby attempts to limit its meaning, he can hardly avoid seeing that, whether expressed in terms of a direct sexual act or in terms of a wider context that would include the act, the present symbol stands for union. It is this sense of the union of all things in a universe of interrelationships that constitutes the first aspect of benevolent necessity in Wordsworth's poetry of the Great Decade.

The word *optimistic* perhaps best characterizes benevolent necessity, because Wordsworth is often able to view the ferment of a changing, finite world from a vantage point removed from the individual finite changes themselves. It is true that this removed view (which may be called transcendental since it rises above the finite) frequently came later than the events and usually depended upon imagination stimulated by outward circumstances and memory; but it came, and Wordsworth felt that its coming was inevitable, the working of a divine providence. It is not true, however, that Wordsworth always looked to the past, using memory and history, or subconsciously induced trance-like visions in order to stabilize and manage feeling by placing it at a distance in space or time.[5] Wordsworth also looked toward the future. In the Prospectus his emphasis is on what is to come, and in lines of 1798-1799 (*Excursion*, IX, 23-26) he has the Wanderer say that "we live by hope / And by desire; we see by the glad light / And breathe the sweet air of futurity; / And so we live, or else we have no life." The future, as well as the past, can furnish Wordsworth with a panoramic scope that reveals an order in the universe. He sometimes moves back from individual things, not to obliterate them from his view nor to lose contact with them, but to see them in the perspective of relationship. Only thus can he see and know that all things are moving together toward perfectibility.

The perspective that Wordsworth sees is one of cosmic benevolence and necessity. Like the philosophic discussions of Godwin and Hartley, his expression of what he sees falls within the general metaphysical world-view that Stephen Pepper calls contextualism.[6] If one is to determine exactly what a man has come to be or what he may become, he must see that man in terms of his past and present context, taking into account all direct and indirect influences. If these influences could not have been other than what they were and if their consequences tend towards moral or social melioration, then we have benevolent necessity in its simplest terms. Furthermore, as a necessity, it is a force working in the universe, and it induces individual man to social benevolence. This definition of benevolent necessity as deterministic meliorative influence seems to be the composite one that Wordsworth developed from his earliest philosophic propensity and from the treatment of benevolence and necessity in the works of Hartley and Godwin. It sees all creation as a oneness composed of interrelationships and reciprocity, one thing shedding sympathetic influence on another in a progressive development.

Because Wordsworth utilized a simple associationism from the time of his earliest poems, the associational philosophy of David Hartley had particular pertinence for him. Hartley devotes his entire first volume primarily to working out his theory of the intricate mechanisms of associationism. His conclusion is that, since associational influences are unavoidable, "man is subject to a necessity ordained by God," and that "if man's actions, and the course of nature, be both fixed, they may be suited to each other in the best possible manner." [7] He states "that nothing is for itself alone," and he finds evidence for this affirmation both in Scripture and in the "mutual relations" of all "the parts of the external world." [8] After an involved algebraic illustration of the associational increase of benevolence, an increase for all "members of the mystical body of Christ," Hartley concludes that thus happiness will "circulate through this mystical body without end, so as that each particle of it would, in due time, arrive at each individual point, or sentient being,

of the great whole, that each would *inherit all things.*" [9]
In this comprehensive mystical body "all things become
comments on each other in an endless reciprocation"
which includes the interrelationships of mental associations.[10] Clearly the conclusions (if not the intricacies)
of Hartley's associational philosophy held an attraction
for someone like Wordsworth, who was also to write of
the interrelationships of a unitary creation.

Although he disclaims following the details of Hartley's "scheme of material automatism," [11] Godwin is in
general agreement with Hartley about the interrelationships that make up the world. He also explains how one
can be aware of this world: "We are able in imagination
to go out of ourselves, and become impartial spectators
of the system of which we are a part." [12] This system is
one of elements linked in such a way that inevitable consequences result. "Every thing in the universe is linked
and united together. No event, however minute and im-
perceptible, is barren of a train of consequences, however comparatively evanescent those consequences may
in some instances be found." [13] Although he qualifies the
term *God,* Godwin can revert to Him in explaining that
this interrelated system of things develops toward good.
"God, according to the ideas usually conceived of that
being, is more benevolent than man, because he has a
constant and clear perception of the nature of that end
which his providence pursues." [14] Nonetheless, man can
partially attain this perception because "mind is a real
principle, an indispensible [sic] link in the great chain
of the universe," and because "every idea, however complex, offers itself to the mind under the conception of

unity." [15] Since "no man stands alone, and can pursue his private conceptions of pleasure, without affecting . . . the persons immediately connected with him, and, through them, the rest of the world," [16] man should be sure that his influence is beneficial. In fact, if one views man in a broad perspective, one sees that his influence can hardly be otherwise, for "the great chain of causes from which every event in the universe takes its rise, has sufficiently provided for the gradual instruction of mankind." [17] The significant thing for man is that he not only is conditioned by the "chain of causes" but also can comprehend its functioning. "Human beings are placed in the midst of a system of things, all the parts of which are strictly connected with each other, and exhibit a sympathy and unison, by means of which the whole is rendered familiar, and, as it were, inmate to the mind." [18] It should now be evident that Godwin's world is one of unitary interrelationships and that man's awareness of this world leads inevitably to tolerance and sympathy [19] because "improvements have long continued to be incessant" and will continue so.[20] It remains only to point out the obvious, that the basis of Godwin's argument is benevolent necessity: it is "the doctrine of necessity [which] teaches us, that all things in the universe are connected together." [21]

As early as 1794, when he was writing additional lines for *An Evening Walk*, Wordsworth had become aware of oneness and interrelationships; [22] and it is not impossible that he learned something of this concept from Godwin's first edition of *Political Justice* in 1793. However, it was not until late 1797 and afterwards that

Wordsworth integrated the idea with his new theme of benevolent necessity. Like the person who can manage to encompass even the multifarious city of London if he "looks / In steadiness" and "hath among least things / An under-sense of greatness; sees the parts / As parts, but with a feeling of the whole" (*Prelude,* VII, 709-712), so Wordsworth can at times express benevolent necessity as a whole by reverting to his conviction that all creation is a oneness of interrelationships. In the lines on the Pedlar added to "The Ruined Cottage" in 1797-1798, Wordsworth says that a "chain of good / Shall link us to our kind" because of the "strange discipline" of nature, natural imagery, and "science." "Thus disciplined / All things shall live in us and we shall live / In all things that surround us." The result is that "thus deeply drinking in the soul of things / We shall be wise perforce, and we shall move / From strict necessity along the path / Of order and of good." [23] When he published *The Excursion* in 1814, Wordsworth diluted this statement to the point of negation by saying *"as if* impelled / By strict necessity" (italics added). [24] But in 1797 there was no qualification. Instead, in "The Old Cumberland Beggar" of that year Wordsworth links to benevolent necessity the concept of interrelationships in terms of the Great Chain of Being:

> 'Tis Nature's law
> That none, the meanest of created things,
> Of forms created the most vile and brute,
> The dullest or most noxious, should exist

Divorced from good—a spirit and pulse of good,
A life and soul, to every mode of being
Inseparably linked.

(lines 73-79)

There is nothing static in this conception of the Chain of Being. Often, as is exemplified by the old beggar, this spirit and pulse of good found in created things is an efficacious force "which to the end of time / Will live, and spread, and kindle" (lines 108-109). Its effectiveness, of course, depends on the fact that necessity has the *modus operandi* of interrelationships and reciprocity through which to work.

It would be tedious to cite all examples of Wordsworth's panoramic view of a benevolent necessity operating through interrelationships, but a few examples will substantiate the fact that it was a consistent Wordsworthian view throughout the Great Decade. In "Influence of Natural Objects" of 1798, writing in the generic first person, Wordsworth identifies benevolent necessity with an *anima mundi* that works primarily through nature:

> Wisdom and Spirit of the universe!
> Thou Soul, that art the Eternity of thought!
> And giv'st to forms and images a breath
> And everlasting motion! not in vain,
> By day or star-light, thus from my first dawn
> Of childhood didst thou intertwine for me
> The passions that build up our human soul;

> Not with the mean and vulgar works of Man;
> But with high objects, with enduring things,
> With life and nature; purifying thus
> The elements of feeling and of thought,
> And sanctifying by such discipline
> Both pain and fear,—until we recognise
> A grandeur in the beatings of the heart.
>
> (lines 1-14)

In the completed 1805 version of *The Prelude* (I, 428-441) Wordsworth used these lines again with no significant changes. The time span between the two almost identical versions is important, for it encompasses most of the Great Decade. But the best known expression of necessity and interrelatedness is found in "Tintern Abbey" (lines 93-102) of 1798.

>                                   And I have felt
> A presence that disturbs me with the joy
> Of elevated thoughts; a sense sublime
> Of something far more deeply interfused,
> Whose dwelling is the light of setting suns,
> And the round ocean and the living air,
> And the blue sky, and in the mind of man:
> A motion and a spirit, that impels
> All thinking things, all objects of all thought,
> And rolls through all things.

One could hardly look for a more thorough statement of necessity, which diffuses through and "impels" all things and which, because of the reciprocal creation between man and nature (lines 106-107), is for man "the guide, the guardian of my heart, and soul / Of all my moral being" (lines 110-111). One finds, however, that this broad sense of an interrelational shaping and tending force is stated or implied in numerous poems up to 1805,[25] and it doubtless lies at the heart of the consolation for change and loss that Wordsworth finally found for concluding the "Intimations Ode" in 1804: addressing the might of things in nature, he says, "I only have relinquished one delight / To live beneath your more habitual sway" (lines 191-192). In regard to time of composition, Wordsworth's last great panoramic statement of this interrelational force of benevolent necessity was given in the 1805 *Prelude*:

> The mind of man is fram'd even like the breath
> And harmony of music. There is a dark
> Invisible workmanship that reconciles
> Discordant elements, and makes them move
> In one society.
>
> (I, 351-355)

This workmanship is possible because of "a soul divine which we participate, / A deathless spirit" (V, 16-17), "a gracious Spirit [which] o'er this earth presides, / And o'er the heart of man: invisibly / It comes, directing those to works of love / Who care not, know not, think not what they do" (V, 516-519). This reverential "Power" "is the very quality and shape / And image of right reason, that matures / Her processes by steadfast laws" (XII, 24-27). In an early manuscript passage which Wordsworth never published is a neat summary of this necessitarian unity: the verse tells of "the one interior life / Which is in all things, . . . that unity / In which all beings live with God, are lost / In god and nature, in one mighty whole" (*Prelude*, p. 525).

Just as Hartley and Godwin (skeptical though he appears) revert to God in trying to explain their concept of benevolent necessity, Wordsworth in the early *Prelude* sometimes does likewise. Nature is the most effective means for the manifestation of benevolent necessity, but "Nature's self . . . is the breath of God" (V, 222). God is "the Giver of all joy" (VI, 614). And it is "Great God! / Who send'st thyself into this breathing world / Through Nature and through every kind of life, / And mak'st Man what he is, Creature divine" (X, 386-389). Thus, though Wordsworth's idea of benevolent necessity is generally philosophic, it also has a religious coloring, which may owe something to Hartley if not to Godwin; it almost certainly owes much to Coleridge, who was always concerned with religion and who doubtless gave a religious cast to his interpretation of Hartley's and Godwin's works when he discussed them with Wordsworth.

Wordsworth, of course, was not a slavish follower of Hartley and Godwin. He found in their works ideas which coincided with his experience and which helped him to synthesize and shape his thinking. He criticized, not the content of Godwin's philosophy (which comprehended both emotion and rationality), but the fact that such philosophic systems were presented in terms of analytic reasoning only. If readers are to be fully influenced by a system of thought, they must have their feelings as well as their reason appealed to. Hence Wordsworth differs from the philosophers in the originality with which he presents the interrelational workings of benevolent necessity in present, real-life-like scenes that everyone can acknowledge as true. It is almost as if Wordsworth turned to the philosophers as the Wanderer turned to the Pastor (*Excursion,* V, 637) and said, "Give us, for our abstractions, solid facts." Wordsworth himself provided the solid facts "by words / Which speak of nothing more than what we are" (Prospectus, lines 58-59).

From the beginning in 1797, Wordsworth writes poems that express the concrete functioning of benevolent necessity through associational interrelationships. The old Cumberland beggar, far from being a useless person, is in reality a "silent monitor" to all who come in contact with him or who merely behold him.

> While from door to door,
> This old Man creeps, the villagers in him
> Behold a record which together binds
> Past deeds and offices of charity,
> Else unremembered, and so keeps alive
> The kindly mood in hearts
>
> . . . . . . . . . . . . . . .
>
> Where'er the aged Beggar takes his rounds,
> The mild necessity of use compels
> To acts of love; and habit does the work
> Of reason; yet prepares that after-joy
> Which reason cherishes. And thus the soul,

> By that sweet taste of pleasure unpursued,
> Doth find herself insensibly disposed
> To virtue and true goodness.
>
> (lines 87-105)

The present-day influence toward virtue and goodness, of which the old beggar is an instance, is not limited to human beings. Although humanity is the main emphasis in this poem, an even wider context is suggested by the fact that the poem begins and ends with references to the small mountain birds that "peck their destined meal" from the crumbs which the beggar's palsied hand is "baffled still" from preventing to fall. Necessity seems to extend its benevolent workings into the relationship between man and the small creatures of nature.

In making a good case for the efficacy of habit in "The Old Cumberland Beggar," Wordsworth further demonstrates an area of general agreement between himself and Godwin. Godwin says that a "man acquires habits ... which he obeys without being able to assign either to himself or others, any explicit reason for his proceeding." [26] In discussing benevolence (he calls it "disinterested action"), he again offers a parallel to Wordsworth's comment in this poem: "Motive may therefore be distinguished, according to its different relations, into direct and indirect; understanding by the direct, that which is present to the mind of the agent at the time of his determination, and which belongs to every voluntary action, and to so much of every action as is voluntary; and by the indirect, that which operates without being adverted to by the mind, whether in the case of actions originally involuntary, or that have become so, in whole, or in part, by the force of habit." [27] However, whereas Godwin generally prefers direct motive, in this poem Wordsworth illustrates the value of indirect motive as a functional element of benevolent necessity.

Other concrete examples of meliorative determinism abound in Wordsworth's poetry of the Great Decade. In overflow lines from "Nutting" Wordsworth writes about the "general ministry" of "Powers" that "with most necessary care / Amid the concentration of your [the nook's] groves / Restore the springs of his [the poet's] exhausted frame." [28] In "Peter Bell" (1798) are similar "Dread Spirits" that sometimes trouble even goodness "for most gracious ends" and effect their "empire" not only "in darkness and the stormy night" but also "when earth is calm, and heaven is bright" (lines 761-780). In the sonnet beginning "It is a beauteous evening" (1802) Wordsworth says that, though his French daughter appears untouched by the scene before her, "the mighty Being is awake," and that Caroline lies "in Abraham's bosom all the year," God being with her "when we know it not." Similarly in the sonnet "To Toussaint L'Ouverture" (1802) there are numerous types of benevolent "Powers" left to carry on L'Ouverture's anti-slavery work; the point is that they *will* do so, as if there were no real alternative. One final instance of concrete influence may be noted. In the motto for "To the Daisy" (1802) Wordsworth significantly substitutes the word *instruction* for *invention* [29] in quoting from George Wither: "from every thing I saw / I could some instruction draw." Within the poem the importance of the daisy is that from it one gains "a happy, genial influence, / Coming one knows not how, or whence, / Nor whither going" (lines 70-72). But Wordsworth usually knows the tendency of such influence. In a second poem entitled "To the Daisy" (1802), the daisy's "home is everywhere" and it has a "function apostolical." In 1843 Wordsworth commented that this term applied to the daisy was used to mean "something sent on a mission; and assuredly this little flower ... may be regarded, in its humble degree, as administering both to moral and to spiritual purposes." [30] The simplest things like a daisy, then, appear to be the operative means of benevolent necessity, working unobtrusively but effectively. They too partake of the "life that breathes not" as Wordsworth affirmed it in "Address to Kilchurn Castle, Upon Loch Awe" (1803): "Powers there are / That touch each other to the quick in modes / Which the gross world no sense hath to perceive, / No soul to dream of" (lines 6-9). These powers are nonetheless at work in concrete, everyday instances, and in the aggregate they compose an interrelated world directed by a benevolent necessity.

Many concrete instances of a personal, intimate sort fill *The Prelude*, a work that may owe more to the stimulation of Godwin and Hartley than has hitherto been noted. While discussing how the characters of men originate in their external circumstances, Godwin says this:

It has been found in the history of several eminent men, and probably would have been found much oftener, had their juvenile adventures been more accurately recorded, that the most trivial circumstance has sometimes furnished the original occasion of awakening the ardour of their minds and determining the bent of their studies.[31]

In a somewhat similar vein of thought, Hartley says:

It is of the utmost consequence to morality and religion, that the affections and passions should be analysed into their simple compounding parts, by reversing the steps of the associations which concur to form them. . . . And as this holds, in respect of persons of all ages, so it is particularly true, and worthy of consideration, in respect of children and youth.[32]

Considering the temporal immediacy of the influence of Godwin and of Hartley on Wordsworth, it seems apparent that statements such as these quoted gave at least as much stimulus to Wordsworth's composing *The Prelude* as did Mark Akenside's incomplete *The Pleasures of Imagination*.[33] What Wordsworth does in *The Prelude* is to examine his past life, beginning with infancy and continuing through youth to manhood while giving special emphasis to juvenile adventures which he calls "spots of time" that "retain / A vivifying Virtue," an "efficacious spirit" (*Prelude*, XI, 258-269). This examination is done in order to see how it was determined for him that he be "a dedicated Spirit" (IV, 341-344) whose life would "express the image of a better time" and who would sing "the law supreme / Of that Intelligence which governs

all" (Prospectus, lines 103, 21-23). Both Hartley and
Godwin admit that finite man cannot perceive all the
directional associative forces in the universe, particularly
all of those that relate to one individual; [34] but man can
know the important ones, and though recognition of
them may come belatedly, that does not lessen their importance. Hartley, for instance, says, "When a person
surveys the events of his past life, he may find many,
which have happened much contrary to natural expec-
tation, and his then desires, which yet appear extremely
beneficial and desirable at the now present time, as also
to have proceeded from natural causes then unknown to
him." [35] It is thus that Wordsworth surveys his past life
in *The Prelude* and finds that nature-induced fear and
even his temporary despair over the French Revolution
all had been working for the good of his development.
In searching the past, however, as Godwin says, "We do
not begin with the successive perception of elementary
parts till we have obtained an idea of a whole; but, beginning with a whole, are capable of reducing it into its
elements." [36] Godwin's wording here is closely similar
to Wordsworth's which was quoted above (*Prelude*, VII,
709-712), though Wordsworth significantly adds "an
under-sense of greatness"; and the procedure advocated
here is the same as that of Wordsworth, who knew well
that it is a "hard task to analyse a soul" (*Prelude*, II,
232). Like the experience in "Tintern Abbey," there are
moments of insight that approach the visionary, moments when "Poets, even as Prophets, each with each /
Connected in a mighty scheme of truth, / Have each

for his peculiar dower, a sense / By which he is enabled to perceive / Something unseen before" (*Prelude*, XII, 301-305). What the poet sees with "deep enthusiastic joy" is "the life / Of all things and the mighty unity / In all which we behold, and feel, and are" (*Prelude*, XIII, 253-255). Beginning with this sense of unity, of the whole, Wordsworth gives in *The Prelude*, as in the numerous short poems that we noted above, many concrete instances of the workings of benevolent necessity.

As Hartley and Godwin admitted, man cannot trace all the determining forces on himself, but he can recall key ones, as Wordsworth does in *The Prelude*. For instance, all the spots-of-time episodes are illustrative of lasting and directional influence: the bird-stealing, boat-stealing, and skating scenes; the vacation walk and the "dedication"; the incidents with the discharged soldier, the drowned man, the blind London beggar, and the gibbet; the dream about the Arab; the news of Robespierre's death; and the experiences at the Chartreuse (in manuscript $A^2$), the Simplon Pass, and the Plain of Sarum. Since the degree of insight and influence pertaining to key moments in life is more important than chronology, *The Prelude* is hardly an autobiography in the usual sense. This fact becomes particularly apparent in the last book of the poem when Wordsworth moves back and forth in past time, recalling the help of Coleridge and Raisley Calvert and dwelling especially on the early time when Wordsworth and Robert Jones climbed Mount Snowdon one summer night in 1791. In prior books Wordsworth tells how "the sweet breath of Heaven" wrought within him "a corresponding mild creative breeze" (I, 41-54), how he was tempered and subdued by objects with which he was "interfus'd" (II, 69-73), how "I felt the sentiment of Being spread" over everything and "in all things / I saw one life" (II, 420-430), and how "life with me, / As far as memory can look back, is full / Of this beneficent influence" (XI, 277-279).[37] The experience on Mount Snowdon in the concluding Book XIII is indicative of what Wordsworth has been illustrating all along. Suddenly breaking through the mist in their ascent, he saw in the level, far-reaching mist a blue chasm from which came the roar of waters. To him the scene was "the perfect image of a mighty Mind,"

> That is exalted by an under-presence,
> The sense of God, or whatsoe'er is dim
> Or vast in its own being, above all
> One function of such mind had Nature there
> Exhibited by putting forth, and that
> With circumstance most awful and sublime,
> That domination which she oftentimes
> Exerts upon the outward face of things,
> So moulds them, and endues, abstracts, combines,
> Or by abrupt and unhabitual influence
> Doth make one object so impress itself
> Upon all others, and pervade them so
> That even the grossest minds must see and hear
> And cannot chuse [sic] but feel.
>
> (XIII, 69-84)

It is thus too that "higher minds" perform. For them "the enduring and the transient both / Serve to exalt; they build up greatest things / From least suggestions" (XIII, 97-99). Even the "grossest minds," however, partake of the "domination" exerted by the force in nature; and if one should examine his past as Wordsworth has done, he would doubtless find key influential events that have necessitated his development, leading ultimately toward moral good.

Wordsworth's description of the Mount Snowdon scene as "the perfect image of a mighty Mind" suggests another facet of Hartleian and Godwinian influence, for both philosophers also used analogies between the human mind and the functioning of the universe. In Hartley's work we find that God, equated with infinite intelligence, is "the inexhaustible fountain, and infinite abyss." [38] Godwin implies the analogy when he discusses the contextualism of the "determination of mind" and immediately says that "every thing is connected in the universe"; mind and matter alike submit to necessity.[39] And his chapter "Of the Mechanism of the Human Mind" immediately follows and analogically relies upon the chapters about the function of necessity in the universe. Fortuity can hardly account for the fact that the poet's image and the philosophers' analogy occur in highly similar ideological contexts.

To conclude the present discussion of benevolent necessity in terms of an interrelated universe, one needs to look at a further aspect that is original with Wordsworth. It is perhaps really an extension of—or the basis

for—his originality in illustrating the force of benevolent necessity in concrete, present-day incidents. In most
of his poetry of the Great Decade, benevolent necessity
is shown working primarily through nature.

Wordsworth found very little in Hartley and Godwin to support his faith in nature. Hartley makes
cursory reference to the "health, tranquillity, and inno-
cence" introduced by actual or contemplated "rural
scenes," and he now and then refers to God as the author
of nature.[40] Once he says, "The moral attributes of God
are to be deduced from observations made upon the
course of nature," [41] but this is only one of the multi-
tudinous analogies that Hartley uses as "proofs" for his
total theory of associationism. By and large, Hartley
turns to religion as his touchstone for explaining benevolent necessity. God has ordained the system of the universe, but He is pretty much the Great Mechanic who
set up the great clockwork of the universe and is now
outside and above it. Hartley's necessity is primarily a
psychological mechanism working through and upon
man; the force that initiated the mechanism is elsewhere.

Godwin can hastily speak of man and "that liberal and
various scene in which nature has permitted him to ex-
patiate," [42] but he sees things of inanimate nature as "phenomena" [43] that make automatic impressions "upon
our organs." [44] In writing of necessity, Godwin's primary
concern is with society, with political government. In
spite of all their discussion of the interrelationship of
things in the universe, both Godwin and Hartley, when
and if they refer to nature, picture it as a mere backdrop

against which man is seen in relation either to a distant God or to the realm of political justice.

Wordsworth's view of nature in relation to man and benevolent necessity is quite different. The difference cannot be seen by juxtaposing passages from the poet and the philosophers. It is to be sensed from a reading of all three writers. One may, however, attempt to describe the difference. To the philosophers the idea of necessitated interrelationships was a theory. To Wordsworth it was a personal fact that he derived from a close communion with nature, a communion traceable from the time of his earliest extant poems and letters. By 1797 Wordsworth was intimate with the salient features of nature through which a panentheistic benevolent necessity can operate. Perhaps the difference lies in the word *panentheistic*. To the philosophers interrelationship was a thought, a rational but theoretical ideal; to Wordsworth it was a conviction of reality derived from experience. There is doubtless irony in the fact that, when Wordsworth reacted to the Wedgwood proposal, his memory of the analyses by Godwin and Hartley provided the help he needed for formulating his new theme of benevolent necessity. While they speculated rationally and scientifically about necessity and interrelationships, he had been experiencing these two phenomena in nature without quite seeing them as one and the same. When, with the help of Hartley and Godwin, insight came to him, he remembered the powerful influence that he had felt and was still feeling from the small form of the daisy to the mightier forms of stars, clouds, mountains, and streams. He wrote of the panentheistic power that he sensed was somehow both beyond and within these forms, a power within them but also "far more deeply interfused." The real difference, then, between the philosophers and Wordsworth is the difference between analysis and synthesis. To the poet everything really was a oneness, moving in inevitable progress.

# FIVE

# Wordsworth's Empirical Teleology

MOST OF WHAT remains to be discussed has already been adumbrated—the process of benevolent necessity, the manner in which it operates, and that towards which it aims—and therefore admits of foreshortened treatment. But a further word should be said about nature before I turn to these facets of Wordsworth's theme.

## MEANS OF BENEVOLENT MINISTRY

Although the positive, beneficial influence of nature is the primary means for benevolent necessity to direct man along the route to moral goodness, nature is not always successful in doing this in Wordsworth's poetry. For instance, in "Ruth" (1799) the "Youth from Georgia's shore" misled and finally deserted Ruth because he had been influenced toward evil by what Wordsworth thought of as the tropic climes of Georgia. Likewise, in

"Peter Bell" (1798) a long intercourse with nature has been ineffective, for "nature ne'er could find the way / Into the heart of Peter Bell"; nature's evil side has combined with the cruel city to generate vice in Peter. Another type of benevolent ministry is necessary to teach Peter a lesson of love and appreciation for others. The natural surroundings are efficacious only in getting Peter lost so that he can come upon a faithful ass (another part of nature) and witness a scene charged with dreadful, supernatural overtones. The obstinate ass not only refuses to be led away; it leads Peter to the side of a pool so that Peter will see its drowned master. While Peter "cannot choose but look; / Like some one reading in a book— / A book that is enchanted," he is so affected and changed that he falls into a trance. As the ass leads Peter to its home, Peter gradually comes to terms with his experience so that when he meets the dead man's widow his heart opens and "he feels what he for human-kind / Has never felt before." We never learn what happens to the youth from Georgia, but for Peter there is a permanent change, as Wordsworth tells us in the final stanza:

> And Peter Bell, who, till that night,
> Had been the wildest of his clan,
> Forsook his crimes, renounced his folly,
> And, after ten months' melancholy,
> Became a good and honest man.

Thus, benevolent necessity does not rely upon only one means of directing man. This is perhaps to be expected in a multifarious universe; otherwise, only nature would be needed to point man toward perfectibility. Since for Wordsworth *nature* is a highly inclusive term, nature is the most effective means. But human relationships and even books, as he tells us in *The Prelude,* also have their part in directing man along the path of good.

### BENEVOLENT NECESSITY AS PROCESS

Wordsworth had seen in his own life the value of other human beings—his mother, Dorothy, Michel Beaupuy, Raisley Calvert, Coleridge, and numerous unnamed ones like wanderers, beggars, and the discharged soldier he encountered one night. But human life, like books and even nature, changes. Books, he tells us in Book V of *The Prelude,* not only can but do decay and perish through change. Generally speaking, however, this kind of change is exceptional in Wordsworth's utterances during the time that he wrote of benevolent necessity. Marmaduke's acceptance of a life filled with remorse and expiation ends *The Borderers* (1796-1797) on a stoic note, and poems like "The Complaint of a Forsaken Indian Woman" (1798) and "The Brothers" (1800) present a stoic and melancholy sense of mutability. But by and large during the Great Decade Wordsworth was convinced of something that endures and is permanent. While Hartley reverted to the religious Godhead for his permanence of a final cause, Godwin relied upon his doctrine of necessity itself for explaining the permanence that belongs to moral truth. Wordsworth, on the other hand, could settle upon no single and established concept as an explanation for permanence. The very fact that he used interchangeably such terms as *power, force, God, presence, something,* and *soul* indicates the difficulty he felt in trying to communicate his idea of permanence. Perhaps he comes nearest to a definition when, in Book V of *The Prelude,* he discusses the "soul divine which we participate" and says that

> Should earth by inward throes be wrench'd throughout,
> Or fire be sent from far to wither all
> Her pleasant habitations, and dry up
> Old Ocean in his bed left sing'd and bare,
> Yet would the living Presence still subsist
> Victorious; and composure would ensue,
> And kindlings like the morning; presage sure,
> Though slow, perhaps, of a returning day.
>
> (V, 29-36)

What is peculiarly Wordsworth's own is his conviction of the infinite extent and ultimate victory of this panentheistic presence. To Hartley and Godwin it is a hope or wish or theory to which they attach a theistic or mechanistic name. To Wordsworth it is an operative fact for which there is the experience but no satisfactory label. He too can give it discursive explanation, but in his poetry he brings it to the reader as it had been brought to him—primarily through experience with an old Cumberland beggar, a daisy, or a spots-of-time in his own life.

Nonetheless, Wordsworth's thought contains a paradox. This "Presence," which is permanent and enduring, is somehow both in and outside of the transient material world. It is permanent as an abstract ideal, yet it is permanent also as a worldly process that could include even a temporary destruction of the world. Through progressive change Wordsworth shows us benevolent necessity at work, and here again he seems to owe something to Hartley and Godwin for the formulation of his thought.

Hartley's idea of God is that of an "inexhaustible fountain" [1] from which everything that flows (including sects, pagan religions, infidelity, atheism, and skepticism) leads finally to God's "infinitely beneficent purposes." [2] From the comprehensive view of God everything is in a process that conducts a changing world inevitably toward the good, since God is all-powerful, all-knowledgeable, and infinitely benevolent. [3] With Hartley this is usually a hope: "There are comfortable hopes, that all evil will be overpowered and annihilated at last, and that it has an entire subserviency to good really and ultimately." [4] This hope is based upon the belief "that all aggregates of pleasure . . . must, from the mechanism and necessity of our natures, and of the world which surrounds us, be made at last to centre and rest upon him who is the inexhaustible fountain of all power, knowledge, goodness, majesty, glory, property, &c. So that even avarice and ambition are, in their respective ways, carrying on the benevolent designs of him who is *all in all*." [5] The finite world develops through associations in such a way that all change (including that

which seems bad to mortals) is really a process of perfectibility.

Omitting only recourse to the Godhead as final cause,
Godwin agrees with Hartley that there is earthly progress through inevitable change. Since "man is in a state
of perpetual mutation," [6] possessing a mind of a "progressive nature" that is characteristically "capable of
improvement," [7] it follows "that mind, as well as matter,
exhibits a constant conjunction of events, and furnishes
all the ground that any subject will afford, for an opinion of necessity." [8] Not only this, but also, because of the
infinite associational influences in the wide context of
the world, "in the events of the material universe, every
thing is subjected to this necessity." [9] Truth will prevail
over error in the final outcome of things, and man, as
well as matter, is thus perfectible through a process of
unavoidable change.[10]

Because he is convinced that in "the system of the universe" nothing terminates in itself but leads "on to an
endless chain of consequences," Godwin says: "In the life
of every human being there is a chain of events, gener-
ated in the lapse of ages which preceded his birth, and
going on in regular procession through the whole period
of his existence." [11] Just such a complicated and infinite
process seems to explain Wordsworth's statement in *The
Prelude* that it is a

> Hard task to analyse a soul, in which,
> Not only general habits and desires,
> But each most obvious and particular thought,

Not in a mystical and idle sense,
But in the words of reason deeply weigh'd,
Hath no beginning.

(II 232-237)

By the time of the 1850 version of *The Prelude* Wordsworth qualified this idea by saying, "If each . . . thought
. . . / Hath no beginning." There was no *if* in 1805.

Neither was there any *if* in the 1797-1798 lines on the
Pedlar, Wordsworth's first indication of his belief that
because of "strict necessity" we move "along the path /
Of order and of good." When in early 1800 he wrote
"Home at Grasmere," the only book he ever did for Part
I of *The Recluse,* Wordsworth said this of human development: "The inward frame / Though slowly opening,
opens every day / With process . . . , / Alternate progress
and impediment, / And yet a growing prospect in the
main" (lines 472-490). This process does not stop with
the individual. Through association it occurs between
people, developing like the old Cumberland beggar's influence, which "to the end of time / Will live, and
spread, and kindle." In "Resolution and Independence"
(1802) Wordsworth's meeting with the old leech-gatherer seemed perhaps "by peculiar grace, / A leading from
above, a something given," and the old man seemed "like
a man from some far region sent, / To give me human
strength, by apt admonishment" (lines 50-51, 111-112).
That admonishment has to do with the idea of change.
Wordsworth had been worrying about the death of poets and the way their lives often changed from gladness

to despondency. What he learned from the brief association with the man was a sense of the man's conti-
nuity as he wandered over the moors, a lesson reinforced
by the man's being likened to a huge stone, a stationary
sea-beast crawled from the ocean, and a cloud that
"moveth all together, if it move at all." The poem, then,
expresses both sides of the paradox about permanence
and change: the old man symbolizes the wholeness of
changing movement which at the same time is as permanent and durable as a huge, motionless stone. Furthermore, the poet himself has been changed to the point of
understanding and accepting the old man's significance;
what at first seemed a dream (line 110) becomes a realized fact in the final stanza. Similar to this poem, "Stepping Westward" (1805) puts emphasis on forward
movement. When asked if he and his fellow traveler are
stepping westward, the poet replies that they are and
that they hardly find themselves in the locale by chance.
In stanza two he says that

> stepping westward seemed to be
> A kind of *heavenly* destiny:
> I liked the greeting; 'twas a sound
> Of something without place or bound;
> And seemed to give me spiritual right
> To travel through that region bright.

If there were any doubt as to what the heavenly destiny
is, the third and final stanza supplies the answer that it
is the advancing process of life. What Wordsworth prob-

ably has in the back of his mind is "the progressive powers . . . / Of the whole species" that he wrote of in the
Prospectus (lines 64-65) and expressed in the "conti-
nental image" of the "Intimations Ode."

Most of our examples of process in Wordsworth's poetry bear resemblance to the progress through association as it is found in Hartley and Godwin. But once
again we must note Wordsworth's difference in his almost constant reference to nature. All the interrelated
necessitarianism pertaining to the old Cumberland beggar occurred as he lived "in the eye of Nature," for "he
is by nature led / To peace so perfect that the young behold / With envy, what the Old Man hardly feels"
("Animal Tranquillity and Decay" of 1797, originally
part of the beggar-poem). In "Tintern Abbey" it is nature's "privilege, / Through all the years of this our life,
to lead / From joy to joy." In fact, the conclusion of the
poem is a reminder to the poet's sister that her development will be directed by nature whether she realizes it or
not. This is the general pattern of what in "Lines Written in Early Spring" (1798) Wordsworth calls "Nature's holy plan." In "To My Sister" (1798) he says that
because of the influence of nature

> We for the year to come may take
> Our temper from to-day.
> And from the blessed power that rolls
> About, below, above,
> We'll frame the measure of our souls . . .

In the poem beginning "Three years she grew," nature is the directive force in Lucy's life:

> Myself will to my darling be
> Both law and impulse: and with me
> The Girl, in rock and plain,
> In earth and heaven, in glade and bower,
> Shall feel an overseeing power
> To kindle or restrain.

Without a multiplying of examples from *The Prelude*, it is plain that nature had overriding importance in Wordsworth's concept of benevolent necessity as a process in this world. It is given no such importance by Hartley or Godwin.

There is, however, one further notable difference between the poet and the philosophers. Wordsworth's most constant natural image for the process of necessary development is that of a river. I am unable to find even the barest hint of this in Hartley, and in Godwin I find only the brief analogy between the flow of a stream and the succession of ideas within a human mind.[12] But for Wordsworth, who spent his infancy within sound of the Derwent and who frequently found and followed streams in his later rambles, the analogy between life and a river was perhaps automatic. Consequently, it is surprising that the symbol has received so little critical mention. Florence Marsh notes that water "is one of Wordsworth's most frequently employed vehicles" and that it dominates *The Prelude*. But she discusses imagery in broad categories—landscape, people, sounds, water, and the like—and her discussion of water [13] gives no treatment of the stream as an image for necessity. Helen Darbishire [14] recognizes the river-image, but she does not discuss its implications. Yet those implications are quite significant, for from 1797 to 1805 Wordsworth found the stream a convenient image for the forward progress due to necessity.

Among fragmentary sketches for the portrait of the Pedlar in "The Ruined Cottage," [15] Wordsworth twice writes of "the mighty stream of tendency" that carries men along with it: "They rest upon their oars, / Float down the mighty stream of tendency / In a calm mood of holy indolence / A most wise passiveness." The old Cumberland beggar has been borne along by "the tide of things" (line 164). In *The Recluse* "the Stream / Is flowing, and will never cease to flow," presenting to the soul whatever

> of outward form
> Can give us inward help, can purify,
> And elevate, and harmonise, and soothe,
> And steal away, and for a while deceive
> And lap in pleasing rest, and bear us on
> Without desire in full complacency,
> Contemplating perfection absolute
> And entertained as in a placid sleep.
> (lines 294-308)

Later in the same work he says that nature "hath dealt with me as with a turbulent Stream, / Some nursling of

the mountains, whom she leads / Through quiet mead-
ows, after . . . / His desperate course of tumult and of
glee" (lines 728-723). In the 1805 *Prelude* one can find
many instances of the stream-image,[16] but I will quote
only the last major one, the one in which Wordsworth
sums up the content of the whole poem, the determining
influences on his own development:

> we have traced the stream
> From darkness, and the very place of birth
> In its blind cavern, whence is faintly heard
> The sound of waters; follow'd it to light
> And open day, accompanied its course
> Among the ways of Nature, afterwards
> Lost sight of it, bewilder'd and engulph'd,
> Then given it greeting, as it rose once more
> With strength, reflecting in its solemn breast
> The works of man and face of human life,
> And lastly, from its progress have we drawn
> The feeling of life endless, the great thought
> By which we live, Infinity and God.
>                              (XIII, 172-184)

This is the river of benevolent necessity, following a
course that may at times meander or even slip under-
ground but inevitably goes forward, directed both
through and by nature. It is a symbol for that life process which has the paradoxical semblance of both change
and permanence, and it seems to have been original with
Wordsworth.

## OPERATIVE MANNER OF NECESSITY

Wordsworth's river symbol is indicative of the manner in which benevolent necessity operates. Incidental changes and impediments (events that seem "evils" at the time) are somehow absorbed or dissolved into the general flow of things; evil is ultimately good and perhaps therefore necessary. Hartley had held this view when he said that everything—pagan religions, atheism, evils, and so on—is part of the benevolent design of God.[17] On the other hand, Godwin, while he discusses this interpretation of necessity in his chapter "Of Good and Evil,"[18] hedges with serious qualifications that show a discrepancy in his thought. He is willing to admit that in a total view of things evil is relative; but he is unwilling to remain complacent about evil, for he feels that some evil is "absolute." He cannot rest content with the "system of optimism" which concludes that everything in the universe is for the best. In order to "escape the error" of such a system, he says, "we must be contented to follow experience, and not to outrun it." We can admit only that there is a mixture of truth in the proposition of optimism and see that "there is a degree of improvement real and visible in the world." Godwin, however, never reconciles his two opposing thoughts about evil; he only leaves the problem standing, unresolved, Janus-like.

Wordsworth seems to have gone beyond even Godwin in explaining away "evil." He simply avoids the subtleties that the argument would involve. The only explicit treatment of the problem that I can find with certainty is put in the mouth of the Wanderer in *The Excursion* (IV, 10-17):

> One adequate support
> For the calamities of mortal life
> Exists—one only; an assured belief
> That the procession of our fate, howe'er
> Sad or disturbed, is ordered by a Being
> Of infinite benevolence and power;
> Whose everlasting purposes embrace
> All accidents, converting them to good.

One cannot be certain when these lines were composed, but the time may have been before 1806. The editors of the text say that Book IV was conceived before Book II, which was completed in 1806, and that perhaps some passages date back to 1798-1800.[19] Whether the quoted passage is among these early ones is not discussed. However, these words help to characterize the Wanderer, who was first called the Pedlar and whose character Wordsworth was working out in 1797-1798; and the idea expressed here coincides with the necessitarian description of the Pedlar's development that has already been examined. The idea in these lines certainly agrees with Hartley's about evil being converted into good, but one can say only that they probably were written during the Great Decade.

Most of the time Wordsworth implies or indirectly assumes that evil is somehow good in the making. This, of course, is part of what was noted on page 14 above as his selective method in justifying "the ways of God to men"; he emphasized the good and what was conducive to good. In the early years of the French Revolution he pictured all events as "a swallowing up of lesser things in great" (*Prelude*, X, 764). When he experienced despair after France and England declared war and after the Jacobins in France committed atrocities in the name of liberty, he turned to that philosophy which stressed rationality and which in turn led to further despair (X, 901). But it was, after all, only a seeming evil, "for, though impair'd and chang'd / Much, as it seem'd, I was no further chang'd / Than as a clouded, not a waning moon" (X, 916-918). The rest of *The Prelude* is devoted to explaining how this and all other apparent retardations were really part of that paradoxical change that is nothing more than permanence: the concluding lines of *The Prelude* refer to the concept of permanence as "this Frame of things / (Which, 'mid all revolutions in the hopes / And fears of men, doth still remain unchanged) . . ." (XIII, 448-450). In other words, even as the mind of man changes and becomes more beautiful and divine, it still exists within that "Frame of things" which is permanent. This conclusion to *The Prelude* should come as no surprise, for in the beginning (I, 355-362) Wordsworth exclaimed:

> Ah me! that all
> The terrors, all the early miseries
> Regrets, vexations, lassitudes, that all
> The thoughts and feelings which have been infus'd
> Into my mind, should ever have made up
> The calm existence that is mine when I

> Am worthy of myself! Praise to the end!
> Thanks likewise for the means!

The means had included apparent "evil."

In order to examine the manner in which benevolent necessity operates, one must look more closely at some of the constituent elements of this means—elements which Wordsworth had already found operative in nature by 1797 but which he developed further. In a broad sense associationism is the basis, as it doubtless is for the fact that all things are interrelated. In one way or another it can account for the monition of natural objects, the influential polarity of natural beauty and fear, and the creative reciprocity between man and nature. Monition is apparent in the "function apostolical" of the daisy, just as it is in the awesome effect of "huge and mighty Forms" such as the cliff in the spot-of-time about the boat-stealing (*Prelude*, I, 372-441). Since man is really a part of nature, he too furnishes monition: the old Cumberland beggar as "silent monitor," the leech-gatherer, the blind beggar of London (*Prelude*, VII, 607-622).

Hartley repeatedly mentioned the efficacy of the fear as well as the love of God.[20] But Wordsworth, whose most constant frame of reference was nature, wrote of the fear and beauty inspired by natural objects, fear and beauty that led to love. He grew up, he tells us, "foster'd alike by beauty and by fear" (*Prelude*, I, 306). The "great mass" of "every natural form, rock, fruit or flower"

Lay bedded in a quickening soul, and all
That I beheld respired with inward meaning.
Thus much for the one Presence, and the Life
Of the great whole; suffice it here to add
That whatsoe'er of Terror or of Love,
Or Beauty, Nature's daily face put on
From transitory passion, unto this
I was as wakeful, even, as waters are
To the sky's motion

(III, 128-136)

These lines and Wordsworth's concern for accurate detail and the "real" language of men in the Preface to *Lyrical Ballads* compare with Hartley's comments on the poet:

It is necessary therefore, that the poet should choose such scenes as are beautiful, terrible, or otherwise strongly affecting, and such characters as excite love, pity, just indignation, &c. or rather, that he should present us with a proper mixture of all these. . . . In all these things the chief art is to copy nature so well, and to be so exact in all the principal circumstances relating to actions, passions, &c. *i.e.* to real life, that the reader may be insensibly betrayed into a half belief of the truth and reality of the scene.[21]

Wordsworth, of course, founded his ideas about the poet and the poet's subject matter more on empirical evidence than on theory; and much of that evidence came from the necessitarian polarity of natural beauty and fear. Even what he calls freedom and "genuine Liberty"

(XIII, 121-122) is actually the molding and enduing "domination" of nature:

> To fear and love,
> To love as first and chief, for there fear ends,
> Be this ascribed; to early intercourse,
> In presence of sublime and lovely Forms,
> With the adverse principles of pain and joy,
> Evil as one is rashly named by those
> Who know not what they say. From love, for here
> Do we begin and end, all grandeur comes,
> All truth and beauty, from pervading love . . .
> (XIII, 143-151)

Discussing the influence of natural beauty and fear leads directly to a consideration of Wordsworth's attitude toward passivity, which is usually ascribed to his knowledge of Hartley. But Hartley's attitude is one of acquiescence to the will of God.[22] Godwin's secular phraseology is closer to Wordsworth's idea. "Man is in reality a passive, and not an active being," writes Godwin.[23] "In volition, if the doctrine of necessity be true, the mind is altogether passive." [24] Neither philosopher, however, relates passivity to the influence of nature as Wordsworth does in works like the Lucy poems, "The Tables Turned," "Lines Written in Early Spring," and "To My Sister." Perhaps the best known lines are those in "Expostulation and Reply" (1798):

> The eye—it cannot choose but see;
> We cannot bid the ear be still;

> Our bodies feel, where'er they be,
> Against or with our will.
>
> Nor less I deem that there are Powers
> Which of themselves our minds impress;
> That we can feed this mind of ours
> In a wise passiveness.

Because of "Eolian visitations," one can hold "unconscious intercourse / With the eternal Beauty, drinking in / A pure organic pleasure," and hence Wordsworth asks when will educators learn "that in the unreasoning progress of the world / A wiser Spirit is at work for us, / A better eye than theirs, more prodigal / Of blessings, and more studious of our good, / Even in what seem our most unfruitful hours?"[25] In these hours of "unfruitful" passivity the benevolent spirit of necessity is at work upon us, and we are creatively active.

Wordsworth's concept does not stop with passivity, however. It includes that reciprocal creation between mind and nature which he says in a note to "Tintern Abbey" he learned from Edward Young. Since Hartley and Godwin assert that all things in the universe are connected through associations, their thought would seem to imply that the human mind, like all other things, participates in the give-and-take of interrelationships. Instead, they go no further than to indicate that the mind can be active within itself or to suggest that one man can be the instigator of motives in others.[26] On the other hand, Wordsworth says this about childhood:

Emphatically such a Being lives,
An inmate of this *active* universe;
From nature largely he receives; nor so
Is satisfied, but largely gives again,
For feeling has to him imparted strength,
And powerful in all sentiments of grief,
Of exultation, fear, and joy, his mind,
Even as an agent of the one great mind,
Creates, creator and receiver both,
Working but in alliance with the works
Which it beholds.
                    (*Prelude,* II, 265-275)

This "auxiliar light" from the mind (II, 387-388) is partly responsible for the fact that "in life's every-day appearances" Wordsworth could "have sight / Of a new world" that has for its base

That whence our dignity originates,
That which both gives it being and maintains
A balance, an ennobling interchange
Of action from within and from without,
The excellence, pure spirit, and best power
Both of the object seen, and eye that sees.
                    (*Prelude,* XII, 369-379)

With the help of Young's thought, Wordsworth was able to make the concept of universal interrelationships more inclusive than did Hartley or Godwin. The manner in which benevolent necessity operates to make good of evil includes natural monition through fear, beauty, and love; but it also includes a creative reciprocity between man and nature. Once again Wordsworth has gone beyond the two philosophers by giving us a more comprehensive synthesis of things.

## PERFECTIBILITY

The goal of benevolent necessity is perfectibility. Hartley believes the attainment will come through a seven-step progression in which each step will combine with those that preceded in order to bring on the next; these steps are sensation, imagination, ambition, self-interest, sympathy, theopathy, and the moral sense. Godwin is not as precise in describing steps to the attainment of moral perfectibility, but morality is the goal of necessity for him also. Man develops through motives which originate outside himself but for which he is somehow also responsible. Virtue is teleological; it consists of utility in terms of the greatest happiness and good for all. Such virtue is progressive in that man is necessarily perfectible and moves from self-love to habitual benevolence—what Godwin calls disinterested action. Since Godwin is aware of the possible anarchic consequences of placing all responsibility on outside motivation, he insists that for man benevolent intention is essential to virtue; but Godwin never clears up this obvious contradiction with anything like satisfaction. He believes in a determinism that allows man to think and choose benevolence, the last perfection of which is "that state of mind, which bids us rejoice as fully in the good that is done by others, as if it were done by ourselves." [27] He can reconcile necessity and man's choosing only by supposing that, as man develops, his preference will have to be benevolence.

Without going into the subtleties of such contradictions, Wordsworth believed that opposites can be and are reconciled into harmony. In his own life he had seen this in terms of the polar influence of natural beauty and fear; he had felt it in regard to both man's passivity and man's reciprocal creativity with nature; and he was convinced that, inasmuch as the human mind was pretty much a mirror of the active universe, all things were reconciled by what he variously called imagination, intellectual love, and right reason. This was the faculty within himself that had been perfectible, but he felt that similar benefit came to everyone, to "souls of humblest frame" (*Prelude,* XII, 15-16). For this reason and to this end, he had written numerous poems about the interrelated associational influences on himself, his sister, Peter Bell, and others. Though man might never reach infinite perfection, he was perfectible because of benevolent necessity; and one could witness the truth of perfectibility from even an old Cumberland beggar through whose influence "the soul" found "herself insensibly disposed / To virtue and true goodness."

# SIX

# Retrenchment from Necessity

AFTER 1805 WORDSWORTH let his theme of benevolent necessity rest, as though he had said all that was to be said about it and did not wish to repeat himself. During the next forty-five years his poetry was occupied with less strict philosophic content. He turned to simplified and often beautiful descriptions of nature, to religion, to a stoical sense of duty which began with "Ode to Duty" in 1804 and was a retrenchment from his former all-pervading theme of necessity. Only fleetingly did he refer to something like benevolent necessity again, and then it was usually part of a definite religious framework or it was referred to for purposes of denial.

It is true that when he published *The Excursion* in 1814 he included earlier written lines about necessity, but by then he had reduced the meaning to supposition only. The Wanderer's development was *as if* by strict necessity. The final 1850 version of *The Prelude* contained changes which suggest that Wordsworth was toning down necessitarian elements in it. For instance, he cut out material on the unifying power inherent to an infant's mental associations [1] and changed some panentheistic lines so that God was no longer the animating force *within* the natural world.[2] This was a loosening of the tight interrelationships through which benevolent necessity had operated.

Once, in *The Friend* (1809), Wordsworth compared the "progress of the species" to that of a winding river and recommended that youth "endeavour to look through the system of his being, with the organ of reason . . . in discovery of the impelling forces and the governing laws." [3] But this is an exception to what can be found in the late poetry. In the sonnet beginning "Who ponders National events" (published 1842) Wordsworth denied that

> the All-ruling Mind,
> With whose perfection it consists to ordain
> Volcanic burst, earthquake, and hurricane,
> Dealt in like sort with feeble human kind
> By laws immutable.

One who believes this is deceived, he said.

One cannot be certain of a reason for Wordsworth's change from a belief in benevolent necessity. The sense of mutability and loss that he had expressed in the "Intimations Ode" may ultimately have been too burdensome for the "philosophic mind" to adjust to. His marriage, the drowning of his brother John, his growing concern for the mental and physical health of Coleridge, his developing friendship with Sir George Beaumont— all of these may have been conducive to changing a liberal optimism to a conservative stoicism. On the other hand, between 1805 and the unknown time when he developed the reactionary attitude of the sonnet just quoted, Wordsworth may simply have felt that too much repetition of a theme was not good for his poetry. Whatever the cause, after 1805 Wordsworth never again gave any sustained poetic development to the concept of benevolent necessity that had been one of his major themes for almost ten years. To a reader who looks at the poet's whole corpus of work, Wordsworth's loss of the theme is regrettable. But such regret diminishes in an overbalance of good. The theme had been an underlying frame of reference for many of the finest poems of the Great Decade. It had helped supply the English-speaking world with some of its greatest literature.

# Appendix

(The following fragmentary essay comes from MS JJ at Dove Cottage, Grasmere, Westmoreland, England. I originally obtained the essay from the late Miss Helen Darbishire, who graciously copied it for me in longhand and assured me that she believed it was "indisputably dictated by William Wordsworth & inscribed by his sister Dorothy, in whose hand it is unmistakably written." Since that time the essay has been published by Geoffrey Little in "An Incomplete Wordsworth Essay upon Moral Habits," *REL*, II, i [1961], 11-13; and it is his transcription which I follow here, reprinting it because it is not yet available in any collection of Wordsworth's prose and because I wish any doubting reader to be able to check the essay against my reading of it. MS JJ, which contains the fragment, dates from 1798-1799 when the Wordsworths were in Germany. The essay is important to the present study of benevolent necessity for two reasons. First, a close reading proves conclusively that Wordsworth is criticizing only Godwin's method of presentation, not the content of his philosophy; nowhere does he say that Godwin rejected feeling as part of man's psychological make-up. Second, the essay is remarkable for discussing and advocating a number of the very aspects of benevolent necessity that Godwin examined in *Political Justice*: the importance of habit, the superiority of the man of benevolence, the desirability of inspiring proper motives in others, the paralleling of self-love with accidental action and of benevolence with necessary action. Without quoting the essay, some critics have referred to it as "proof" that Wordsworth was opposed to Godwin in 1798-1799. Instead, the essay demonstrates that, even while he deplored the ineffectiveness of Godwin's analytic method of writing, Wordsworth was in real agreement with the content of Godwinian thought.)

I THINK PUBLICATIONS in which we formally and systematically lay down rules for the actions of men [? man] cannot be too long delayed. I shall scarcely express myself too strongly when I say that I consider such books as Mr Godwyn's Mr Paley's and those of the whole tribe of authors of that class as impotent to all their intended good purposes, to which I wish I could add that they were equally impotent to all bad one[s]. This sentence will, I am afraid be unintelligible. You will at least have a glimpse of my meaning when I observe that our attention ought principally to be fixed upon that part of our conduct & actions which is the result of our habits. In a strict sense all our actions are the

result of our habits,—but I mean here to exclude those
accidental and indefinite actions, which do not regularly and in common flow from this or that particular
habit. As, for example a tale of distress is related in a
*mixed company*, relief for the sufferers proposed. The
vain man, the proud man, the avaricious man &c., all
contribute, but from from [sic] very different [motives
*del.*] feelings. Now in all the cases except in that of the af-
fectionate and benevolent man I would call the act of giving more or less accidental—I return to our habits—
Now I know no book or system of moral philosophy
written with sufficient power to melt into our affections,
to incorporate itself with the blood & vital juices of our
minds, & thence to have an influence worth our notice
in forming those habits of which I am speaking. Perhaps
by the plan which these authors pursue this effect is
rendered unattainable. Can it be imagined [that *del.*]
by any man who has deeply experienced his own heart
that an old habit will be foregone or a new one formed
by a series of propositions, which, presenting no image to
the mind can convey no feeling which has any connection with the supposed archetype or fountain of the
proposition existing in human life. These moralists attempt to strip the mind of all its old clothing when
their object ought to be to furnish it with new. All this
is the consequence of an undue value set upon that faculty which we call reason. The whole secret of this jug-
gler's trick [? trickery] lies, not in fitting words to things
(which would be a noble employment) but in fitting
things to words—I have said that these bald and naked
reasonings are impotent over our habits, they cannot

form [? force] them, from the same cause they are equally powerless in regulating our judgments concerning [*the* -*ing is written over something else*] & [*presumably Wordsworth forgot to delete the* &] the [*the* 'e' *of* the *is written heavily and drawn out to alter* things *to* the] value of men and things. They contain no picture of human life they *describe* nothing. They in no respect enable us to be practically useful by informing us how men placed in such or such situations will necessarily act, & thence enabling us to apply ourselves to the means of turning them into a more beneficial course, if necessary, or of giving them new ardour & new knowledge when they are proceeding as they ought.

We do not *argue* in defence of our *good* [actions *misspelt and del.*] actions we feel internally their beneficent effect; we are satisfied with this delicious sensation and even when we are called upon to justify our conduct we perform the task with languor & indifference. Not so when we have been unworthily employed; then it is that we are all activity & keenness, then it is that we repair to systems of morality for arguments in defence of ourselves, & rare [? rash] enough are we to find them. In this state of our minds lifeless words, & abstract propositions will not be destitute of power to lay asleep the spirit of self-accusation & exclude the uneasiness of repentance. Thus confirmed & comforted we are prepared immediately to transgress anew, & following up this process we shall find that I have erred when I said that [Here the essay ends abruptly as five pages have been torn from the Notebook.]

# Notes

## CHAPTER ONE

1. George Wilbur Meyer, "Wordsworth: An Appreciation," *Tulane Studies in English*, III (1952), 28, but see pp. 11-31 *passim*. See also Meyer's *Wordsworth's Formative Years* (Ann Arbor, 1943), pp. 244-245 and 248-249.

2. See James Volant Baker, *The Sacred River: Coleridge's Theory of the Imagination* (Baton Rouge, 1957), pp. 17 and 19-20; and Hoxie Neale Fairchild, *Religious Trends in English Poetry* (New York, 1949), III, 273-275, 277, 281, 286, and 293-294.

3. Coleridge's letter to Thomas Poole, 15 January 1804; *Collected Letters of Samuel Taylor Coleridge*, ed. Earl Leslie Griggs (Oxford, 1956), II, 1037.

4. *The Complete Works of William Hazlitt*, ed. P. P. Howe (London, 1932-1934), XX, 60.

5. *Ibid.*, XI, 17.

6. *Ibid.*, XI, 106.

7. See *The Collected Writings of Thomas De Quincey*, ed. David Masson (London, 1896), II, 289-293.

8. See Arnold's preface to *Poems of Wordsworth* (London, 1920), p. xix.

9. Melvin M. Rader, *Presiding Ideas in Wordsworth's Poetry*, Univ. of Wash. Pubs. in Lang. and Lit., VIII, No. 2 (Seattle, 1931), p. 123.

10. Quoted in *The Poetical Works of William Wordsworth*, ed. Ernest de Selincourt and Helen Darbishire, 5 vols. (Oxford, 1940-1949), V, 364, hereafter cited as *Poetical Works*. References to Vols. II and III will be to the second editions of 1952 and 1954 respectively.

11. Emile Legouis, *The Early Life of William Wordsworth, 1770-1798*, trans. J. W. Matthews (New York, 1932), p. 266.

12. Arthur Beatty, *William Wordsworth: His Doctrine and Art in Their Historical Relations*, Univ. of Wis. Stud. in Lang. and Lit., No. 24 (Madison, 1922), p. 31; see also pp. 109, 119, 242, and 271.

13. *Ibid.*, p. 35.

14. Rader, "The Transcendentalism of William Wordsworth," *Modern Philology* (MP), XXVI (1928), 169-190.

15. Rader, *Presiding Ideas*, p. 169; see also pp. 122-123.

16. Fairchild, *The Romantic Quest* (New York, 1931), p. 360.

17. Fairchild, *Religious Trends*, III, 189; see also pp. 152, 161, and 181.

18. Darbishire, "Wordsworth's Belief in the Doctrine of Necessity," *Review of English Studies* (RES), XXIV (1948), 121-125.

19. Darbishire, *The Poet Wordsworth* (Oxford, 1950), p. 163, but see pp. 161-163 *passim*.

20. William Wordsworth, *Poems in Two Volumes, 1807*, ed. Helen Darbishire (Oxford, 1952), pp. vii-lii.

21. For additional brief references see Joseph Warren Beach, *The Concept of Nature in Nineteenth-Century English Poetry* (New York, 1956), pp. 13, 23, 42, 47, 119, and 159; H. W. Garrod, *Wordsworth: Lectures and Essays*, 2nd ed. (Oxford, 1927), p. 84; Earl Leslie Griggs, "Wordsworth Through Coleridge's Eyes," pp. 45-90 in *Wordsworth: Centenary Studies Presented at Cornell and Princeton Universities*, ed. Gilbert T. Dunklin (Princeton, 1951), pp. 51 and 52 n.; George McLean Harper, *William Wordsworth: His Life, Works, and Influence* (New York, 1916), II, 77-78; E. D.

Hirsch, Jr., *Wordsworth and Schelling: A Typological Study of Romanticism* (New Haven, 1960), pp. 108-114; John Jones, *The Egotistical Sublime: A History of Wordsworth's Imagination* (London, 1954), pp. 40 and 114-115; and Mary Moorman, *William Wordsworth, A Biography: The Early Years, 1770-1803* (New York, 1957), pp. 380-381.

## CHAPTER TWO

1. Since specific footnotes cannot suggest the extent of my reliance upon certain books, I should like to single out the following as most helpful in my formulation of scientific and metaphysical background: Beach, *Concept of Nature*; E. A. Burtt, *The Metaphysical Foundations of Modern Science* (New York, 1955); Arthur O. Lovejoy, *The Great Chain of Being: A Study of the History of an Idea* (Cambridge, Mass., 1936); Alfred North Whitehead, *Science and the Modern World: Lowell Lectures, 1925* (New York, 1956); and Basil Willey, *The Eighteenth Century Background: Studies in the Idea of Nature in the Thought of the Period* (London, 1949), and *The Seventeenth Century Background: Studies in the Thought of the Age in Relation to Poetry and Religion* (New York, 1955).

2. Wordsworth's "Tintern Abbey." See Beach, pp. 47-109; and Ben Ross Schneider, Jr., *Wordsworth's Cambridge Education* (Cambridge, Eng., 1957), pp. 68-69 and 166.

3. For instance, see Newton's letter to Bentley, printed by Burtt, pp. 288-290.

4. Whitehead, pp. 10-39.

5. Willey, *Seventeenth Century Background*, p. 158.

6. Fairchild, *Religious Trends*, II, 551-552, and III, 12.

7. Beach, pp. 90-91.

8. See the quotation in Newton P. Stallknecht, *Strange Seas of Thought: Studies in William Wordsworth's Philosophy of Man and Nature*, 2nd ed. (Bloomington, Ind., 1958), p. 135.

9. See Fairchild, *Religious Trends*, III, 29.

10. Schneider, pp. 168-169.

11. See Beach's "Note on Wordsworth's Reading" in *Concept of Nature*, pp. 569-577. See also Z. S. Fink, *The Early Wordsworthian Milieu: A Notebook of Christopher Wordsworth with a Few Entries by William Wordsworth* (Oxford, 1958); except for some prose works like the Lake District guidebooks, poetry is what the early Wordsworthian milieu reflects.

12. Fairchild, *Religious Trends*, II, 485-486.

13. *Ibid.*, I, 189-201.

14. *Ibid.*, II, 211.

15. *Ibid.*, II, 304.

16. *Ibid.*, I, 468.

17. Quoted by Fairchild, *ibid.*, I, 499, but see pp. 499-509 *passim*. See also Willey, *Seventeenth Century Background*, p. 293, on Pope's "optimistic 'philosophy.' "

18. Fairchild, *Religious Trends*, I, 521-525.

19. References and quotations are from *The Complete Works of James Thomson*, ed. L. Logie Robertson (London, 1908). This benevolent spirit that "impels" and "agitates the whole" often recurs in Thomson; see, for examples, "Summer," lines 32-42, 182-184, 318-341, 1660-1663; "Winter," lines 579-587; and *The Castle of Indolence*, II, xlvii. There is a similar impelling force in Wordsworth's "Tintern Abbey."

20. References to and quotations from *The Complaint; or, Night Thoughts* are from *The Poetical Works of Edward Young* (London, 1852), Vol. I.

21. References and quotations are from *The Poetical Works of Mark Akenside*, ed. Rev. Alexander Dyce (Boston, 1864).

22. References and quotations are from *The Poetical Works of James Beattie* (Boston, 1863).

23. See Fairchild's summation of the development of the belief in *Religious Trends*, II, 373.

24. The fact that this date is later than Wordsworth's probable first acquaintance with Godwin's and Hartley's works is discussed in Chapter Three below.

25. Meyer, *Wordsworth's Formative Years*, p. 5.

26. *The Early Letters of William and Dorothy Wordsworth* (*1787-1805*), ed. Ernest de Selincourt (Oxford, 1935), pp. 34-35, hereafter cited as *Early Letters*.

27. Schneider, pp. 112-163.

28. See Meyer, *Wordsworth's Formative Years*, p. 89.

29. *Early Letters*, p. 55.

30. Wordsworth's letter to the Bishop of Llandaff, "Apology for the French Revolution, 1793" in *The Prose Works of William Wordsworth*, ed. Alexander B. Grosart (London, 1876), I, 6, hereafter cited as *Prose Works*.

31. *Early Letters*, p. 164.

32. See *Poetical Works*, I, 10 and 13.

33. *Early Letters*, p. 84.

34. *Ibid.*, p. 4.

35. *Ibid.*, pp. 18 and 22.

36. *Ibid.*, pp. 25, 29 and n.

37. *Ibid.*, p. 58.

38. For example, see *ibid.*, pp. 74-76.

39. Quoted in *ibid.*, p. 138 n.

40. *Ibid.*, p. 145.

41. For example, in addition to the instances noted in the present text, see "The Vale of Esthwaite," lines 95-102, 153-162, and 498-513; much of the Alpine letter of 1790 (*Early Letters*, pp. 34-35); all of the sonnet "Sweet was the walk"; and part of the 1791 letter to Mathews (*ibid.*, p. 55).

42. Beatty, pp. 99-102.

43. Meyer, *Wordsworth's Formative Years*, pp. 48 and 170 n.

44. For a discussion of Wordsworth's emphasis on "the ministry of fear" in poems later than "The Vale of Esthwaite," see Raymond Dexter Havens, *The Mind of a Poet: A Study of Wordsworth's Thought* (Baltimore, 1941), I, 39-53.

45. Rader, "The Transcendentalism of William Wordsworth," pp. 181-190.

46. *Poetical Works,* I, 9.

47. *Ibid.,* p. 10.

## CHAPTER THREE

1. David V. Erdman, "Coleridge, Wordsworth, and the Wedgwood Fund," *Bulletin of the New York Public Library,* LX (September and October 1956), 425-443 and 487-507.

2. This letter is new evidence from the unpublished Abinger Collection at Duke University; the letter is now published in *ibid.,* pp. 430-433.

3. See *Early Letters,* p. 164.

4. See Erdman, pp. 498-503. On the dating of the lines see also Meyer, "The Early History of *The Prelude,*" *Tulane Studies in English,* I (1949), 134 n.

5. See Francis E. Mineka, *The Dissidence of Dissent: The Monthly Repository, 1806-1838* (Chapel Hill, 1944), p. 239.

6. See Meyer, *Wordsworth's Formative Years,* pp. 48 and 170 n.; see also Schneider, p. 109, who suggests that Wordsworth learned of Hartley at Cambridge.

7. Willard L. Sperry, *Wordsworth's Anti-climax* (Cambridge, Mass., 1935), p. 126.

8. Fairchild, "Hartley, Pistorius, and Coleridge," *Publications of the Modern Language Association (PMLA),* LXII (1947), 1013-1014 n.

9. *The Complete Poetical Works of Samuel Taylor Coleridge,* ed. Ernest Hartley Coleridge (Oxford, 1912), I, 110 and 123.

10. For a detailed discussion of necessity in the story of the Mariner, as well as for further cogent argument that Coleridge's shift from necessity to transcendentalism did not come until 1799, see S. F. Gingerich, "From Necessity to Transcendentalism in Coleridge," *PMLA,* XXXV (1920), 1-59. For argument that the poem is not necessitarian, see Robert Penn Warren, "A Poem of Pure Imagination: an Experiment in Reading," in *Selected Essays* (New York, 1951), pp. 198-305, particularly 223-224, 227, and 290-291; War-

ren's essay was originally published with an edition of "The Rime of the Ancient Mariner" in 1946.

11. *Wordsworth's Formative Years*, pp. 238-239 n.

12. I am indebted to Professor Patton and Duke University and to Lord Abinger for allowing me to use these dates. Mary Moorman has utilized the dates in her biography, but not in connection with the theme of benevolent necessity.

13. Again I am indebted to Professor Patton, Duke University, and Lord Abinger for this information.

14. William Godwin, *Enquiry Concerning Political Justice and Its Influence on Morals and Happiness*, variorum ed., 3 vols., ed. F. E. L. Priestley (Toronto, 1946), I, 433, hereafter cited as *PJ;* all references to Godwin's three editions are from this variorum edition.

15. *Ibid.*, I, 426-427.

16. *Ibid.*, I, 436.

17. *Ibid.*, I, 363.

18. *Ibid.*, I, 371.

19. *Ibid.*, I, 363, but also pp. 361-397 *passim.*

20. *Ibid.*, I, 93.

21. *Ibid.*, I, 451.

22. *Ibid.*, I, 452.

23. *Poetical Works*, II, 385.

24. See *ibid.*, IV, 400-404.

25. *Early Letters*, p. 156.

26. *PJ*, II, 512-513.

27. For instance, see B. Sprague Allen, "Analogues of Wordsworth's *The Borderers*," *PMLA, XXXVIII* (1923), 267-277; Beatty, pp. 188-189; Norman Lacey, *Wordsworth's View of Nature: And Its Ethical Consequences* (Cambridge, Mass., 1948), p. 41; and Legouis, pp. 253-319 and 397-402.

28. De Selincourt, "Early Readings in *The Prelude*," *London Times Literary Supplement*, No. 1,554 (12 Nov. 1931), p. 886.

29. F. W. Bateson, *Wordsworth: A Re-interpretation* (London, 1954), p. 121.

30. See the Preface, *Poetical Works*, II, 392. Since Wordsworth's fragmentary essay is not readily accessible, I have included it in an appendix so that one can check the essay against my reading of it. See pp. 121-124.

31. On this interpretation of *The Borderers*, see F. M. Todd, *Politics and the Poet* (London, 1957), p. 88.

32. Discussed by Meyer, *Wordsworth's Formative Years*, pp. 189-190.

33. *PJ*, II, 325, 499-500; I, 390; and II, 496.

34. Allen, "William Godwin and the Stage," *PMLA*, XXXV (1920), 369.

35. See Coleridge's *Biographia Literaria*, ed. John Shawcross (London, 1907), I, 59.

36. Willey in *Eighteenth Century Background*, pp. 212 and 235; Priestley in *PJ*, III, 12 and 87-94.

37. Allen, "William Godwin as a Sentimentalist," *PMLA*, XXXIII (1918), 1-29.

38. Cited by Meyer, *Wordsworth's Formative Years*, p. 185.

39. *PJ*, II, 538.

40. *Ibid.*, III, 337-338.

41. See Stephen's essay "Godwin and Shelley" in *Hours in a Library* (New York, 1907), III, 357-406, especially 371-376; see also the comment from Stephen's *English Thought in the Eighteenth Century* as quoted by Meyer, *Wordsworth's Formative Years*, p. 185.

42. Legouis, p. 312.

43. *PJ*, I, 81.

44. *Ibid.*, I, 308.

45. *Ibid.*, I, 311-312. See also p. 421, where "feelings and ideas" join in the government of moral conduct.

46. *Ibid.*, III, 321-331.

47. *Ibid.*, I, xxiii.

48. *Ibid.*, I, xxvi. See also II, 146 and 341.

49. *Ibid.*, I, 376. See also p. 57.

50. *Ibid.*, II, 269.

51. *Ibid.*, II, 373.

52. William Wordsworth, *The Prelude, or Growth of a Poet's Mind*, ed. Ernest de Selincourt, 2nd ed., rev. Helen Darbishire (Oxford, 1959), p. 418. This and all subsequent references, unless otherwise noted, are to the 1805 version and to this edition.

53. For example, de Selincourt, *Prelude*, p. 605, but see pp. 603-606 *passim*.

54. Meyer, *Wordsworth's Formative Years*, pp. 153-170.

55. On Wordsworth's relation to Roman Stoicism, see Jane Worthington, *Wordsworth's Reading of Roman Prose* (New Haven, 1946), pp. 43-74. For Godwin's views, see *PJ*, II, 9-10, 363-364, and 377.

56. For example, see Godwin's "Summary of Principles," *PJ*, I, xxiii and xxv.

57. *Ibid.*, I, 395-396 and 430.

58. *Ibid.*, II, 521-523.

59. See *ibid.*, II, 191-208, 283-296, and 388.

60. *Ibid.*, I, 111-119.

61. *Ibid.*, I, 449-451. For a discussion of eighteenth-century optimism, see Lovejoy, "Optimism and Romanticism," *PMLA*, XLII (1927), 921-945.

62. See Meyer, *Wordsworth's Formative Years*, pp. 8-11.

63. *PJ*, I, 18-19. Compare Wordsworth's letter to the Bishop of Llandaff (1793) in *Prose Works*, I, 3-23.

64. *PJ*, II, 397-413.

65. For example, see Beatty, pp. 96, 188-189; and Oscar James Campbell, *Sentimental Morality in Wordsworth's Narrative Poetry*, Univ. of Wis. Stud. in Lang. and Lit., No. 11 (Madison, 1920), pp. 46-47. Since Legouis is primarily responsible for the anti-Godwinian criticism of Wordsworth, see also *Early Life*, pp. 253-319 and 397-402, but especially 304-315.

66. See Beatty, p. 188, for instance.

67. *PJ*, II, 423.

68. *Ibid.*, II, 432-437.

69. Legouis, p. 314.

## CHAPTER FOUR

1. David Perkins, *The Quest for Permanence: The Symbolism of Wordsworth, Shelley, and Keats* (Cambridge, Mass., 1959), pp. 1-100, particularly 12-31. See also David Ferry, *The Limits of Mortality: An Essay on Wordsworth's Major Poems* (Middletown, Conn., 1959).

2. Havens, I, 39-53.

3. *Prelude*, I, 153, 370, 494, 624.

4. Perkins, pp. 14-16. See Alan Grob's corrective essay, "Wordsworth's 'Nutting,'" *Journal of English and Germanic Philology (JEGP)*, LXI (1962), 826-832.

5. Perkins, p. 40, but see pp. 39-53 *passim*.

6. Stephen C. Pepper, *World Hypotheses: A Study in Evidence* (Berkeley, 1942, 1957), pp. 232-279.

7. David Hartley, *Observations on Man, His Frame, His Duty, and His Expectations* (London, 1791), I, 508, hereafter cited as *Observations*.

8. *Ibid.*, II, 182; but see also pp. 286-287 and 290.

9. *Ibid.*, II, 287 (Hartley's italics).

10. See *ibid.*, II, 306, 343, and 417.

11. *PJ*, I, 400 n.; see also pp. 399 and 405.

12. *Ibid.*, I, 427.

13. *Ibid.*, I, 42; see also pp. 160, 401; II, 388.

14. *Ibid.*, I, 318.

15. *Ibid.*, I, 386 and 414.

16. *Ibid.*, I, 442.

17. *Ibid.*, III, 306.

18. *Ibid.*, II, 127.

19. See *ibid.*, I, 392.

20. *Ibid.*, I, 451.

21. *Ibid.*; see also p. 452.

22. See *Poetical Works*, I, 9, 10, 12-13, and 16.

23. See *ibid.*, V, 400-403.

24. *Excursion*, IV, 1268-1270.

25. See "Peter Bell," lines 141-145; "Expostulation and Reply," lines 17-28; "The Tables Turned," lines 15-25; "Lines Written in Early Spring," lines 5-6, 11-12, 19-20, 22; "To My Sister," lines 27-36; the Prospectus to *The Excursion,* lines 21-22, 52-58, 64; "Michael," lines 28-33; "Hart-Leap Well," lines 163-168.

26. *PJ,* I, 65-66.

27. *Ibid.,* I, 431.

28. *Poetical Works,* II, 505.

29. See the note in *ibid.,* II, 491.

30. *Ibid.,* IV, 414.

31. *PJ,* I, 46-47; see also pp. 160 and 370, and II, 512-513, on the individual's right to a naturally evolved education.

32. *Observations,* I, 81. Part of my discussion immediately following only gives details to some generalized conclusions about Hartleian influence that Professor Beatty (pp. 48, 107, 109, 288) drew forty-three years ago when he examined associationism and the "three ages of man" in Wordsworth's poetry. Professor Beatty, however, denies (p. 19) the influence of Godwinian doctrine; one thing I wish to point out is the similarity of that doctrine to Hartley's in reference to associationism. Either or both philosophers' comments could have stimulated Wordsworth in the writing of *The Prelude.* Finally, my present discussion of *The Prelude* points out what Beatty's discussion of necessity (p. 31) did not—that many elements in *The Prelude* illustrate the work of a benevolent necessity.

33. Abbie Findlay Potts, *Wordsworth's* Prelude, *A Study of Its Literary Form* (Ithaca, 1953), pp. 256-263, suggests that Wordsworth consciously took over Akenside's unfinished task of "the secret paths of early genius to explore."

34. For example, see *Observations,* I, 369, 502; II, 17, 44; and *PJ,* I, 372, 407.

35. *Observations,* II, 44.

36. *PJ,* I, 407.

37. Of many other similar instances in *The Prelude,* see I, 271-285; II, 237-280; VIII, 624-640, 770-823; the MS variants of X, 190-192, on the "stern necessity" and "Providence of Heaven" that

returned Wordsworth to England after his second journey to France; and the MS variants given in de Selincourt's notes, pp. 525 and 613-614.

38. *Observations*, I, 296, 497; and II, 9-13, 32.

39. *PJ*, I, 160 and 368.

40. *Observations*, I, 420 and 460.

41. *Ibid.*, II, 185.

42. *PJ*, I, 289.

43. *Ibid.*, I, 363.

44. *Ibid.*, I, 382.

### CHAPTER FIVE

1. *Observations*, I, 497.

2. *Ibid.*, II, 195.

3. *Ibid.*, II, 28, but pp. 13-30 *passim*.

4. *Ibid.*, II, 105.

5. *Ibid.*, I, 463.

6. *PJ*, I, 245.

7. *Ibid.*, II, 231, 299.

8. *Ibid.*, I, 368.

9. *Ibid.*, I, 364.

10. *Ibid.*, I, 86-95.

11. *Ibid.*, I, 401-402, 384.

12. *Ibid.*, I, 409.

13. Florence Marsh, *Wordsworth's Imagery: A Study in Poetic Vision* (New Haven, 1952), pp. 91-96.

14. Darbishire, "Wordsworth's Belief in the Doctrine of Necessity," pp. 121-125.

15. See *Poetical Works*, V, 413.

16. For instance, see *Prelude*, MS 18a variant, p. 42; II, 214-215; III, 10-12, 339-343, 508-510; IV, 39-55, 110-111; V, 183-184; VI, 672-678; VII, 5-13, 615-616; IX, 1-9; X, 150-153, 770-772; MS variant, p. 426; MS variants, pp. 462-463; XIII, 57-65, 365-367.

17. See *Observations*, I, 305; II, 105, 195, 213, 372, 386, and 433. Hartley's German interpreter and commentator, Pistorius, emphasized this facet of Hartleian necessity; see III, 556 and 661.

18. *PJ*, I, 439-463.

19. *Poetical Works*, V, 423.

20. *Observations*, I, 419, 466, 489; II, 320-321, 325.

21. *Ibid.*, I, 431.

22. See *ibid.*, I, 470, 509; II, 48, 196.

23. *PJ*, I, 389.

24. *Ibid.*, I, 403.

25. *Prelude*, I, 104, 589-591; V, 384-388. See also XII, 1-14, and lines from the Alfoxden notebook on p. 566.

26. For instance, see *Observations*, I, 368-373; and *PJ*, I, 390.

27. *PJ*, I, 438.

## CHAPTER SIX

1. Compare the two versions, *Prelude*, pp. 56 and 57.

2. Again compare *ibid.*, pp. 388 and 389, 496 and 497.

3. *Prose Works*, I, 313 and 320.

# Index